MW01634841

GREAT
VANCOUVER

GREAT VANCOUVER

An Indispensable Guide to Places to Go and Things to Do in the Lower Mainland

From the
10 Great Lists in

Whitecap Books
Vancouver/Toronto

Copyright © 2000 by *The Province*
Whitecap Books
Vancouver/Toronto

All rights reserved. No part of this publication may be reproduced, stored
in a retrieval system, or transmitted in any form or by any means, electronic,
mechanical, photocopying, recording or otherwise, without prior written
permission of the publisher.

The information in this book is true and complete to the best of our
knowledge. The author and publisher disclaim any liability in connection
with the use of this information. For additional information, please contact
Whitecap Books, 351 Lynn Avenue, North Vancouver, BC V7J 2C4.

Edited by Leanne McDonald
Proofread by Elizabeth Salomons
Cover and interior design by Lisa Eng-Lodge

Printed and bound in Canada

Canadian Cataloguing in Publication Data

Great Vancouver

Copublished by: Vancouver Province
Includes index.
ISBN 1-55285-143-5

1. Vancouver (B.C.)—Guidebooks. I. Province (Vancouver, B.C.: 1956)
FC3847.18.G73 2000   917.11'33044   C00-910665-0
F1089.5.V22G73 2000

The publisher acknowledges the support of the Canada Council for the Arts
and the Cultural Services Branch of the Government of British Columbia for
our publishing program. We acknowledge the financial support of the
Government of Canada through the Book Industry Development Program
for our publishing activities.

For more information on this and other Whitecap titles,
please visit our website at www.whitecap.ca

CONTENTS

INTRODUCTION

By Jonathan McDonald, Take a Break Editor

Welcome to Vancouver! Okay, now that we've got the pleasantries out of the way, let's get down to business.

You've arrived. The city is beautiful. The mountains, the ocean, the streets and the gorgeous parks blow you away.

That's all fine and dandy, but other than those little pamphlets the concierge at the hotel lends you, you don't have a clue what to do while you're here.

That's where we can help. A year ago, the Entertainment and Lifestyles staff at *The Province*, British Columbia's best-read daily newspaper, realised that what was lacking was a weekly guide to all those things we love about this city, its suburbs and outlying areas. We knew that people love to plan their weekends and love to hear suggestions, but we wanted to pick places and things to do that are timeless.

And so were born the Ten Great lists.

It was easy to come up with ideas that would suit both tourists and readers alike. Places to tube and toboggan? Definitely. Things to do with the kids on a rainy day? Of course. Great movie theatres, great nature walks, great beaches, pools, places to walk your dog? Please, do tell. And then there are at least ten first-class shops within an hour's drive that sell virtually nothing but candy. (Yeah, we know you don't like candy, but we provided our insight anyway.)

We've learned a lot in the past year. We've learned that if you want a great street to walk down, there's more to Vancouver than Robson Street or Water Street—the ones that most visitors head to because they're easy and obviously tourist-friendly. We've learned that if you want to go for a lovely nature walk, Stanley Park's a wonderful place to go, but it will be full of every single visitor from out-of-town. We came up with a bunch more parks—some of which, we promise, you'll practically have to yourself.

We also discovered that if you want to go to a drive-in, there's only one left in the entire area. Or that if you step inside the Hollywood Theatre on West Broadway, you might as well be stepping back in time to the 1930s. And if you need to go somewhere to clear your mind—a great idea after a day of your senses being assaulted—you'd do well to head to the gritty part of downtown, where the Dr. Sun Yat-Sen Classical Garden sits in meditation among the noise and the poverty.

You may not think you need to turn to us for guidance. But we think you'll be happy to expand your horizons. Visitors and Vancouverites alike tend not to explore. It's easy in a big daunting world to keep doing the same old thing: dinner on Robson Street, a movie on Granville, drinks down in Gastown, a hike up the Grouse Grind, a stroll around the Granville Island Market, or an ice cream at Baskin Robbins.

If you're in town on a Thursday, pick up *The Province.* Or log onto our website at www.vancouverprovince.com. You'll see that we continue to publish our weekly Ten Great lists, and that there's way more to the Vancouver area than meets the eye.

The Ten Greats, it seems, can go on in perpetuity—we seem to be blessed with a remarkably diverse climate and culture. And if we start running out of ideas? Then, frankly, we wouldn't be in the right business.

Enjoy the lists. *Province* reporters Dana Gee, Tom Harrison, Hardip Johal, Mike Roberts, Glen Schaefer, David Spaner, Judy Swanson and I have had a lot of fun coming up with them.

Welcome to Vancouver.

GREAT REASONS TO LOVE VANCOUVER

BY DANA GEE

I t's inevitable. Vancouverites can't help bragging about their city. Can you blame us?

Sure, we occasionally complain about the rain, the high mortgages, traffic...but what city doesn't have its pet peeves? All that negativity is washed away with the rain when you take a close look at where we call home.

To celebrate this great place to live in and to help you plan to make the most of Vancouver and the Lower Mainland, we've come up with some lists that will take you on tours from the ten best dog walks to the ten best pumpkin patches in the Lower Mainland. And what better way to kick off the book than a list of ten great reasons to love Vancouver and the Lower Mainland?

NORTH SHORE MOUNTAINS: Cypress, Grouse and Seymour—a sure-fire hat trick for recreational fun, not to mention the fabulous views they afford those who feel a stroll around Stanley Park's Lost Lagoon is getting back to nature. From secret mountain bike trails to high alpine hikes, these beauties win for scenery, terrain and accessibility.

STARBUCKS AT ROBSON AND THURLOW: This is the perfect people-watching point. For greater enjoyment, make a game out of the viewing. Try to match the leather jacket with the motorbike. Eavesdropping potential is massive. If it isn't an actor talking about how he impressed producer Chris Carter, it's a rock star wannabe and her manager wannabe fawning over each other's hair.

STRAWBERRY FIELDS FOREVER: Well, at least for the summer months. In-between Langley and Aldergrove on Highway 1 lies sweet, red heaven with field upon field overflowing with berries. Most of these farms are U-Pick, meaning that you pay for what you pick. A quick tip from those in the know: The eat one, pick one technique doesn't go over well with the growers.

FIFTH AVENUE CINEMAS: Wonderful films that are pretty much free of the Hollywood hype and no signs of any ice cream pail-sized popcorn tubs with propaganda emblazoned on them. This Vancouver cultural hot spot also boasts free parking. The Fifth Avenue Cinemas are located at 2110 Burrard Street.

KITSILANO AND WRECK BEACHES: In a city of excellent beaches, these two stand out. Kitsilano Beach (affectionately known as Kits Beach to locals) is a hive of activity during the summer months. For the active types, there's tennis, outdoor basketball, beach volleyball and Kits pool. For the more laid-back types, the beach is blanket-ready. Excellent people-watching opportunities if your eyes aren't already peeled to your summer reading. Just be aware that dark sunglasses are a must. Kitsilano Beach is located along Cornwall Avenue in Vancouver.

Wreck Beach is your opportunity to shed society's restricting uniforms and join the nude beach-goers. Clothing is optional here, and the atmosphere is very non-judgemental. This is the place to truly hang loose. It's not people-watching friendly, though, so keep your eyes to yourself. Wreck Beach is located off NW Marine Drive on the University Endowment Lands.

CLOVERDALE RODEO: Yee-haa! Complete with top-notch bull riding and long neck beers, this world class rodeo is a real hoot. If you really want to get into the spirit of things, cowboy boots, tight jeans and big belt buckles are de-riguer. To make a drive out of it, take scenic Highway 17 west to Cloverdale and stop at the fruit stands along the way.

PROXIMITY: As in close to many cool places, such as Whistler, Vancouver Island and the Gulf Islands. The only downside is the long weekend exodus leaves highways and ferry line-ups looking like a sports utility vehicle convoy experiment gone bad. A word to the wise: If you're travelling with BC Ferries, spend the extra money for a reserve boarding ticket. It's worth it.

BRACKENDALE: Check out this area of the Squamish River during January and February when the transient population hits down. Calling this area home are not errant skiers unable to find lodging up the road at Whistler, but rather, the grand-daddy of all birds of prey, the bald eagle. Thousands and thousands of these massive creatures have moved down from Alaska to decorate the trees lining the river. For the best view, check out a guided raft journey down the river. To get to Brackendale, follow the Sea-to-Sky Highway toward Whistler.

WEATHER: Vancouver's climate allows for year-round recreation. Ski in the morning, tennis in the afternoon. It's like something out of a *Fantasy Island* script, except for the morality play. In this part of the country, proof of citizenship consists of a Mountain Equipment Co-op membership and a roof rack. Activities from angling to windsurfing are mere moments away and are year-round. For vicarious thrills, check out Mountain Equipment Co-op's store at 130 West Broadway.

 **STANLEY PARK:** Yes, this is an easy choice, popular with residents and tourists alike. But we've narrowed our favourite part down to the wooded trails that are fringed by the seawall. Flora and fauna abound around Bear Lake. The soft rustic paths make for quiet walks, free of teetering, flailing beginner inline skaters. Stanley Park is located west of downtown Vancouver. It is accessible off Georgia Street toward the Lions Gate Bridge.

GREAT NATURE WALKS

Is it possible to come up with a list of the ten best nature walks in Vancouver and the Lower Mainland? The thought occurs as the weather starts getting warmer, the rain slicker is put away and the legs come out from under long pants. With woods, water and mountains in everyone's backyard, any list of ten will leave out someone's favourite walk. So remember, this is a list of ten "great," not necessarily "best" walks.

For suggestions not covered here, check out any number of hiking guides for walks around the Lower Mainland.

STAWAMAS CHIEF: Did you know that the 652-metre-high cliff (approximately 1/3 of a mile) near Squamish is the second-largest granite outcropping in the world? The biggest one is Gibraltar. Apart from being one of the world's choice rock-climbing destinations, with some 280 climbing routes up the cliffs, the Chief also has three easy hikes to the top, all starting at the end of the dirt road two kilometres (just under a mile) south of Squamish. As a bonus, the view includes the

wind-surfers to the west in Howe Sound. To get to the
Stawamas Chief, take Highway 1 north toward Squamish.

GOLD CREEK, GOLDEN EARS PROVINCIAL PARK:
From the public lot at the end of the road, there's an easy
walk up to the falls, which is a great place to stop for lunch.
The view of the river and snow-capped mountains are spectacular. For more serious hikers, there are more strenuous
trails beyond the falls. To get to Golden Ears Provincial Park,
take Highway 1 east to Dewdney Trunk Road. Turn left on
232nd Street, and right on Fern Crescent.

DEAS ISLAND REGIONAL PARK: Watch the rowing club
practise as you stroll along beside the south arm of the Fraser
River. The walk takes you over the top of the Massey Tunnel.
There's lots of room for horseback riding if you feel like
going for a trot rather than a walk. The spectacular scenery
includes huge eagles' nests and a great view of the barges
and tugboats hard at work. Deas Island Regional Park is
located off Highway 99 between Richmond and Delta.

STANLEY PARK: So you don't want to go too far from your
favourite coffee shop for your nature fix? Try the trails east of
Third Beach, which pass by some of the biggest trees in the
city. For a more sedate stroll, try following the Seawall all the
way around back to a well-deserved latte on Denman Street.
Stanley Park is located in the West End of downtown
Vancouver off of Georgia Street.

UNIVERSITY ENDOWMENT LANDS/PACIFIC SPIRIT
PARK: Sprawling between a university, a golf course and
Vancouver's Point Grey homes are this forested network of
more than 35 kilometres (approximately 22 miles) of trails.
On a sunny day, there's nothing to remind you of how close
you are to the city, except for the steady flow of bikers, hikers and horseback riders. If it's solitude you're seeking, try
the park on a rainy day. The Park Centre on 16th Avenue has
trail maps. The University Endowment Lands/Pacific Spirit
Park are located at the west ends of NW Marine Drive, 4th
Avenue West, 10th Avenue West and 16th Avenue West.

PITT RIVER DIKES: This walk has it all: migrating water-fowl, alders, cottonwoods, maples, farmland and mountain views all on a long, flat walk. It's the perfect walk for starting off in the late afternoon on a sunny spring day and returning on the homeward stretch by the light of a gorgeous sunset. To get to the Pitt River Dikes, head north on Dewdney Trunk Road in Pitt Meadows, just east of the Pitt River Bridge. Turn left at Harris Road to a parking lot across a bridge. Then start walking west along the Alouette Slough toward the Pitt River.

BADEN-POWELL TRAIL: This 50-kilometre (26-mile) daisy-chain of footbridges and paths spanning the North Shore mountains from Deep Cove to Horseshoe Bay is really a collection of trails—a greatest hits of nature walks. Boy Scouts built the final links to the trail more than 30 years ago and any one of several chunks would make a good day's walk. It touches part of the Grouse Grind for the more aggressive walker, and passes by Cleveland Dam and Hollyburn Ridge. Depending on how much of the trail you tackle, be aware of where you're going and when nightfall comes. More than a few hikers have been stranded overnight when daylight ended before their walk did. You can access the east end of the trial at the end of Capilano Road in North Vancouver, or the west end by taking the Eagleridge Exit (Number 2) off Highway 1 in West Vancouver.

FISHTRAP CREEK TRAIL: Walks of varying length are possible, with the longest being about an hour. There's a gravel path for those on foot and a paved path for inline skaters, baby strollers and kids on bikes. There's a bird sanctuary as well that people can see but can't get to, and islands on the creek that are home to a variety of animals. Fishtrap Creek Trail is located on MacClure and Old Yale Road in Abbotsford. Take Exit 83 off of Highway 99.

REIFEL BIRD SANCTUARY: This combination of gravel paths and wooden walkways leads through a huge waterfowl habitat. Observation towers placed strategically throughout the marshes enable birdwatchers to get a better view. Great blue herons, bald eagles and red-winged blackbirds are

among over 240 species of birds that have been sighted. The Reifel Bird Sanctuary is located at 5191 Robertson Avenue on Westham Island in Ladner. Call 946-6980 for more information.

LIGHTHOUSE PARK OR SEYMOUR DEMONSTRATION FOREST: We went back to the North Shore and couldn't pick between West Vancouver's waterfront Lighthouse Park, where a walk through the towering trees can be combined with bird watching, rock climbing and driving, or North Vancouver's Seymour Demonstration Forest, which offers a choice between many scenic trails and a paved road—closed on Saturdays—to accommodate baby strollers, inline skaters and more timid cyclists. Head up Lillooet Road to the Seymour Demonstration Forest or west on Marine Drive to Lighthouse Park.

GREAT PLACES TO JOG

By Hardip Johal

You can run amok, run along, run off at the mouth, be run ragged, run the show, run wild—or you can just plain run some of the most inviting trails in the Lower Mainland.

We may have mentioned this a few times before, but Vancouver and the Lower Mainland is a recreational paradise, and whether you're a marathon master or a 20-minute miler, you won't find jogging any better than this.

STANLEY PARK SEAWALL: Call us obvious, but the Stanley Park Seawall is a gem. Start at the Aquatic Centre down in False Creek or at the base of Denman Street across from Milestone's or at the Vancouver Rowing Club. Head through the park, clockwise or counterclockwise, and bask in the never-dull vistas: Kitsilano and UBC, the North Shore and Lions Gate Bridge, and one of the neatest angles on downtown. You can make a good 10 kilometres (approximately 6 miles) out of this, but beware of inline skaters and dogs on long leads. Best time to run on weekends? Early morning, long before the crowds discover it.

SPANISH BANKS: Call this the anchor run. Start from Brock House down on Point Grey and follow the gravel trail along the beach to the anchor monument at Spanish Banks. On any given weekday evening, you'll find running groups packing the trail. The route takes the average runner 20 minutes each way. The surroundings are scenic beyond belief—both on the way out, with the water and mountains, and on the way back, as the distant city grows closer. The only traffic is foot traffic, it's pretty easy on the knees, and there are washrooms and water stations. But don't run it at night when the light is poor.

ENDOWMENT LANDS: The UBC Endowment Lands feature the most amazing network of soft woodchip trails. This is the perfect cross-country antidote to the pounding you'll take on pavement anywhere else. Keep your bearings and learn the trails—it's a huge, heavily forested area that can be downright confusing. Things to be careful of: roots jutting out of the ground, cyclists and night-time, when the trails become scarier than a bad horror movie.

COQUITLAM: *Province* reader Shirley McQuillan, who leads a jogging club out of the Running Room in Coquitlam, recommends the PoCo River Trail and the North Trail. You can run up to 16 kilometres (10 miles) on the first and 10 kilometres (approximately 6 miles) on the North PoCo Trail, which is McQuillan's favourite. "It becomes more rugged as you go further up, where there are more stumps and rocks," she says. For mastering the tricky terrain, you will be rewarded by the beautiful sight of Crystal Waterfalls, says McQuillan. The North PoCo Trail begins just past Westwood Street off Lougheed Highway, as does the PoCo River Trail.

The Running Room is a chain of stores dedicated to joggers. The Running Room in Coquitlam is located at 11118 Ponderosa Street.

STANLEY PARK: For those who can't abide the crowds or hard surface of the Seawall, there are trails that offer more serene surroundings within Stanley Park. A particularly great one is the Beaver Lake Trail. Use common sense and avoid running in wooded areas on your own.

DELTA: Rob Leickner, manager of the Running Room in Surrey, says his club's favourite nearby route is a 10 kilometre (one-way) trail (approximately 6 miles) that begins under the Alex Fraser Bridge in Delta (near the Side Track Pub on River Road). The first section of the run, called the Burns Bog Trail, takes joggers to the Delta Watershed at 64th Avenue. From there, the second section of the trail, called the Delta Watershed Trail, takes runners around the Delta Golf Course to Colebrook Road. "It's a shaded trail and you take less pounding than you would on the road," says Leickner. The Running Room in Surrey is located at 410-7380 King George Highway.

NORTH VANCOUVER: Rob Leickner may manage a runners' store in Surrey, but as personal favourites go, his trail of choice is the 50-kilometre (approximately 31-mile) Baden–Powell Trail in North Vancouver, which can be accessed from the base of the Grouse Grind in North Vancouver. The trail is quite technical and more for experienced runners than beginners. It's well marked with signs indicating mileage and location. Once again, use common sense and let people know where you're headed and when you expect to return.

DOWNTOWN VANCOUVER: The bridge-to-bridge run is a beauty. Start in Yaletown and head southbound on the Cambie Bridge's nice wide sidewalk. Then take the spiral staircase down to the False Creek seawall. Head west on the winding sidewalk past the various condo develop.ments and Granville Island to the Burrard Street Bridge. Pop onto the bridge and head back into downtown. Finish the run on the north side of False Creek and get a celebratory juice at Urban Fare at the base of Davie Street.

NORTH SHORE: For scenic splendour and an uphill work-out, head for the Cap Pacific Trail, which takes joggers from Ambleside over quaint log bridges, past Cleveland Dam to the base of Grouse Mountain. At this point, super-humans can opt to do the Grouse Grind or head onto the Baden–Powell Trail (see number 7). For the other 99.9 per cent of us, rest, reclining and refreshment is a must at this point.

LANGLEY: Langley resident and *Province* reader Monica Torgerson does her walking and running on Houston Trail, a 4-kilometre (approximately 1.5-mile) circuit near popular Derby Reach. "It's very green and quiet and has both hilly and flat areas," says Torgerson. Houston Trail is about a seven-minute drive along 96th Avenue, just past Fort Langley.

GREAT VIEWS

BY GLEN SCHAEFER

We're suckers for a great view, and this place has enough of them to give any of us pause at least once a day. There's nothing like turning an ordinary-looking corner and happening on a vista that just takes your breath away. Fortunately, Vancouver and the Lower Mainland offer an abundance of views, so there's more than enough to share. In the interests of research, we drank in a few of them and came up with ten great views around the Lower Mainland. Enjoy!

GROUSE MOUNTAIN: Yes, it can be tough for newcomers to keep their eyes on the snow on a sunny day at this North Shore Mountain. This is a scene that is Olympian in the mythical sense, where a body can get to feeling like one of the Pantheon gods while taking in the view from Surrey to the Gulf Islands. If you want to pass the Skyride on Grouse Mountain, drive your car most of the way up nearby Cypress

Mountain and stop at the lookout there. This view is equally impressive by night. To get to the peak of Grouse Mountain, take the Grouse Mountain Skyride at the base of the mountain, located at the northern terminus of Nancy Greene Way in North Vancouver. To get to Cypress Mountain, take Exit 8 off of Highway 99.

THE REVOLVING RESTAURANTS: Cloud Nine atop the Empire Landmark Hotel on Robson has a piano bar and a restaurant, neither of which would suit children with small attention spans. This one's for silver-wedding anniversaries, long talks with young adults about how the world's their oyster, or affairs between 60-year olds. A revolution in this restaurant takes in everything from Georgia Straight to Mount Baker. The Cloud Nine restaurant and the Empire Landmark Hotel are located at 1400 Robson Street.

A crow's fly away, at the Lookout atop Harbour Centre, there's a kid-friendly observation deck on one level and a swish restaurant above. The observation level has coin-operated binoculars pointing in all directions. The attraction here is the glass-walled elevator that zips from street level to the top in one gut-dropping swoop. The admission price for the elevator lets you ride all day. Restaurant patrons ride free. Harbour Centre is located at 555 West Hastings.

VANCOUVER AQUARIUM: It seems odd to go indoors for a great view, but this one is truly fantastic. If you go downstairs and stand in front of the big, thick glass, you'll get a view that looks back at you. Those belugas seem to be equally curious about who's on the other side of the glass. For the best "viewing" time, go on a weekday when it's just you and those big, white mammals. The Vancouver Aquarium is situated in Stanley Park.

ANY TREE-LINED VANCOUVER STREET DURING BLOSSOM SEASON: These are found views—those unexpected soul-lifters that greet you as you turn a corner. A local favourite is at the corner of 7th Avenue and Spruce Street in the Fairview Slopes neighbourhood—the city seems to be ringed by a garland of spring colours. Others include the view from Trimble Park at 8th Avenue and Trimble Street, and various points along 16th Avenue in the Point Grey neighbourhood. From the top of the hill at Knight Street and 36th Avenue, you can see all of the city and the North Shore. Or stand next to the Captain Vancouver statue in front City Hall and follow his gaze down Cambie Street.

SUNSET BEACH: At sunset, of course. Spend the earlier part of the day taking in everything else Stanley Park has to show, and end your day here with a colour light show. Again, this venue is quite crowded on weekends, so we suggest a weeknight for optimal viewing. Sunset Beach is located along Beach Avenue in Vancouver.

THE TOP OF BURNABY MOUNTAIN: From this vista, it appears that the whole Lower Mainland is spread out like a quilt. This constant awe-inspiring view is the perfect setting for one of Vancouver's two universities—Simon Fraser University. One has to wonder, though, how the students can possibly tear their eyes off the view and get any studying done? To reach the summit of Burnaby Mountain and the Simon Fraser University Campus, turn off the Gaglardi Way exit on the Lougheed Highway.

HEADING NORTH ON THE LIONS GATE BRIDGE: Drivers have to keep their eyes glued to the stop-and-go of the traffic, but passengers can raise their gaze from the bridge up to the fog-draped hills and mountains in front, cruise ships sliding underneath, and water on both sides. Switch drivers for the trip back—the view coming in to Stanley Park is just as good, if not better, especially if there's a sunset.

LIGHTHOUSE PARK IN WEST VANCOUVER: If you're perched on the rocks on the west side of the park, you can watch BC Ferries trundle past. If you sit quietly, the odd seal will come up to investigate your presence. This is an excellent picnic spot, and no matter how many people you meet on the trails, you're almost guaranteed a quiet spot to have to yourself. Lighthouse Park is located on Marine Drive in West Vancouver.

PACIFIC SPIRIT PARK: If you head just 100 metres (approximately 90 yards) into any of the trails of Pacific Spirit Park, you're immediately engulfed in green. Variations on the colour surround you as far as your eyes can see. So thick is the forest, you almost feel like leaving a trail of breadcrumbs. Although you're geographically located within the city, the city itself disappears. Pacific Spirit Park is located along NW Marine Drive in Vancouver.

HEADING INTO VANCOUVER IN THE WINDOW SEAT OF A JET COMING OFF THE POLAR ROUTE FROM EUROPE: The daunting, unimaginably vast wilderness and mountains, followed by a look over Harrison Lake, solves the mystery of why so many people are entranced with Vancouver and the Lower Mainland. As the plane nears the airport, this place suddenly unfolds like a lotus beneath you.

GREAT RAINY DAY ACTIVITIES FOR KIDS

By Hardip Johal

It's too grey and drippy to go outside and the kids are showing signs of cabin fever. You don't want to watch TV, and you seem to have gone through the selection of videos that are both entertaining and suitably rated. If you're from out of town, your wonderful vacation in Vancouver is in danger of being washed down the drain. Traipsing to the usual tourist destinations in the rain isn't too kid-friendly, but the hotel doesn't have much to offer in the way of entertainment. Before you tear out your hair, here are ten great rainy day activities for kids.

1 BUILD AN INDOOR FORT: Whether you're stuck in a hotel room or in your home, there's always suitable material at hand. Few things delight children more than having their own private little world, so give them some sheets, string and a helping hand. Throw in some snacks, a sleeping bag and maybe a flashlight and you'll be surprised at how long they can entertain themselves by camping out indoors.

STORY TIME: Pick a great book—choose one above your youngster's reading level—and read aloud to the kids. For a great selection of children's books, try Vancouver Kidsbooks at 3083 West Broadway. For a truly literary experience, however, check out the children's section of the Vancouver Public Library located at 350 West Georgia.

CUPCAKE ART: Whip up some cupcakes, then supply your kids with frosting, candies, sprinkles and other edible decorations, and let them explore their artistic sides. This activity isn't as messy as you might think, as long as you limit the work space to the kitchen table or a single counter.

LET THE GAMES BEGIN: The ultimate arcade, Playdium at Eaton Centre Metrotown, offers everything from interactive soccer and baseball games to outer-space battles, so let the games begin! Be forewarned, however, this recreation is not cheap, and those with a low noise threshold should be aware that loud music and sound effects are part of the Playdium experience. Eaton Centre Metrotown is located at 4700 Kingsway in Burnaby.

HEAD TO THE BEACH...INDOORS: There's a lot to be said for artificial beaches like the one at Newton Wave Pool, which features two great water slides. Admission is relatively cheap, you can stay as long as you want, and lifeguards are there to keep an eye out. Okay, so there's no sunshine or shells to collect. On the other hand, you won't come home with a sunburn or sand in your swimsuit. Newton Wave Pool is located at 13730-72nd Avenue in Surrey.

CRASH CRAWLY'S ADVENTURE FUN CENTRE: The ultimate antidote to couch-potato disease, this Coquitlam fun centre is a giant indoor playground with oversized apparatus. You can climb, slide, jump and laugh to your heart's content. Crash Crawly's Adventure Fun Centre is located at 1-1300 Woolridge, off Lougheed Highway in Coquitlam.

GO PUDDLE SPLASHING: Who says you have to stay inside when it rains? Grab your kids, boots and raincoats, and go out and have fun. A walk along the Stanley Park Seawall is a lesson in the awesome forces of nature. And the best thing about being in a rainy climate is that you don't have to look too hard to find a puddle to splash in. The streets won't be crowded, so it's the ideal time to explore and find that perfect hot chocolate to ward off the chill.

VISIT THE AMAZON: Along with juicy hamburgers (and more sophisticated fare for adults), the Rainforest Café serves up alligator, gorillas and parrots…not literally, of course. The creatures are part of the wild décor. Diners eat amidst a profusion of rainforest vegetation and to the accompaniment of jungle sounds. There's even a recurring thunderstorm. Kids will get a kick out of the ear-wagging elephant, tree-shaking gorilla and the real-live tropical fish in the giant aquarium. The Rainforest Café is located in Eaton Centre Metrotown at 4700 Kingsway in Burnaby.

BUILD A MINIATURE THREE-DIMENSIONAL CASTLE: For patient, detail-oriented kids, 3-D puzzles are a new twist on an old pastime. Hardly a snap to do, a 3-D puzzle can keep kids busy for numerous cold, soggy days. To keep what should be a fun, challenging activity from becoming an exercise in frustration, choose a puzzle that's appropriate for your child's age and ability.

THROW AN UN-BIRTHDAY PARTY: Take a lesson from the Mad-Hatter and the March Hare. Who says you have to wait for a birthday to celebrate? Bake a cake, show your kids how to make a party hat and wrap some tiny treats. Our favourite source for party favours is a dollar store, where everything is just a loonie.

GREAT RAINY DAY ACTIVITIES FOR ADULTS

By Mike Roberts

Unfortunately for visitors and residents alike, spring in Vancouver is almost synonymous with rain. Vancouverites don't lovingly refer to it as "the Wet Coast" for nothing. Depressing? Well, it doesn't have to be. Step out of your rainy day blahs and shake off that rising damp with any one of these ten great rainy day activities for adults.

HOTEL LOBBIES: Walking into the lobby of a swank hotel is like walking through the gates of an embassy—officious minions march about in uniform, desk aides shuffle papers, and unless you're waving a banner, everyone ignores you. The hotel lobby is a rainy-day, people-watching haven. For the ultimate in lobby elegance, visit the Hotel Vancouver. This city landmark is a favourite among movie stars like Ben Affleck. You never know who you might spot. The Hotel Vancouver is located at 900 West Georgia.

THE QUAYS: From quay to shining quay, the Lower Mainland is blessed with two of the niftiest market malls in all of North America. The New Westminster Quay Public Market, a hop, skip and an overpass from the New West

SkyTrain station, features two floors of stores (30 little shops), the Paddlewheeler Pub (affectionately referred to as the Paddlewhacker by the locals) and a riverboat-style casino docked next to the tugboats on the working arm of the Fraser River. Recommended: Touch of Africa (unusual carvings, trinkets and colourful clothing); Alpine Bakery (treats and staples, always fresh); and the two Chinatown-style grocery stalls at either end.

The Lonsdale Quay Market, at the north end of a SeaBus ride, features 50 shops selling everything from beads, soap and popcorn to First Nations and Celtic arts and fashions. The fish markets are spectacular. For a tasty treat, head to the food fair area and grab a Beaver Tail, a truly Canadian treat made with fried dough, sugar and lemon juice. It tastes better than it sounds…trust us.

BOWLING: Gather the crew, break out the sanitized lace-ups, a pencil and scorecard and hit the lanes. Bowling fades in and out of fashion, but for an afternoon of cheap laughs at the expense of your less co-ordinated associates, nothing beats a few frames on the lanes. Five-, ten-pin, just like riding a bike. But these days, alleys are going the extra mile of hardwood to lure bowlers in from the dreary world beyond their doors. The Commodore Lanes and the Varsity-Ridge 5 Pin Bowling Centre are staples of the sport in Vancouver, but outfits like Grandview Bowling Lanes on Commercial Drive and Lucky Strike Lanes in New West offer light and sound shows, and, get this, Glow-in-the-Dark-Bowling! The Commodore Lanes are located at 838 Granville Street. The Varsity-Ridge 5 Pin Bowling Centre is located at 2120 West 15th Street. The Grandview Bowling Lanes are located at 2195 Commercial Drive, and the Lucky Strike Lanes are located at 1205-6th Avenue North in New Westminster.

TRAIN RIDES: When the rain starts in, get the train out of town. What better time to settle down for a ride on a fully sheltered conveyance? The expensive version of the rainy day train ride—the Cariboo Prospector—takes you out of North Vancouver's rain belt up to Whistler. Contact BC Rail for rates and schedules at 984-5246. For a day on the trains on the cheap, hop aboard the eastbound Westcoast Express and enjoy the dry ride to Mission. Contact 683-7245 for more information.

TOP OF VANCOUVER REVOLVING RESTAURANT:
When the fog and drizzle sets down and you're feeling lower than a slab of rain-soaked sidewalk, why not rise above it all with a trip to the top of the Harbour Centre Tower? That's right, rise above the cloud line and hunker down with a special coffee or two in the round-about restaurant. Look down on the less fortunate as they battle against the wet and their wind-popped umbrellas. Have another special coffee. You deserve it. Harbour Centre is at 555 West Hastings.

VANCOUVER PUBLIC LIBRARY: We usually go to the
library when we need to. You know, to see how far we've moved up the reserve list for Madonna's coffee table sex book, or if we need some background on car maintenance, patio repairs or the War of 1812. But—and this is true—the library can actually be a lot of fun if you've got a few rainy-day hours to kill. People-watching aside (and you get some colourful types in the public libraries), write down all those questions and big words you've been meaning to look up and go for it, or just take in the amazing architecture. The Vancouver Public Library is at 350 West Georgia.

YAOHAN CENTRE: For the ultimate Asian experience on
the wet West Coast, take a day trip to the Yaohan Centre on No. 3 Road in Richmond. This mega-mall of all things exotic is bound to boost those rainy-day spirits. Fill your boots with Korean, Vietnamese, Taiwanese or Chinese food for under five bucks a plate in the food fair. Fill your baskets with wild (as in, "What the heck is that thing?!") fruits and vegetables. (Don't forget to ask for cooking/peeling instructions.) Fill your skin with pins at the acupuncture booths. It's cheap, it's fun and it all originated in a much sunnier part of the world. Yaohan Centre is located at 3700 No. 3 Road in Richmond.

REP HOUSES: When you've got a rainy afternoon to kill, a movie or two or three is a sure-fire cure-all for the winter blahs. Trouble is, movies, even matinees, are pricey when you're looking at a long-haul triple bill. The solution? The Rep House. These movie halls may feature films from last summer, but how can you go wrong at $2.99 or $5.99 for three big-screen experiences. Girlfriend won't watch sci-fi? Here's your chance to catch up that must-see flick that you missed on its first run. Boyfriend flatly refuses another date movie? Sneak away to a Merchant-Ivory triple bill. Vancouver offers a few rep houses. A local favourite is the Ridge, located at 3131 Arbutus Street.

NEWTON WAVE POOL: You're wet. Why not get wetter? Stop fighting it and dive in. The Newton Wave Pool ought to do the trick. We've already recommended this one to people who have to entertain children on rainy days (see previous list), but who says kids get to have all the fun? Head on over when the kids—squealing line-up jumpers all—are in school, and have yourself a ball with the water blasters and dual super slides. And when you're done, don't bother drying your hair. The wet look won't turn heads 'round these parts this time of year. The Newton Wave Pool is located at 13730-72nd Avenue in Surrey.

DR. SUN YAT-SEN CLASSICAL CHINESE GARDEN:
Continuing with the theme of getting wet when it's wet, take an afternoon out of the water-logged rat race and enter that calm pool of Zen known as the Dr. Sun Yat-Sen gardens in Chinatown. Ah, the symmetry. Ah, the balance and the inner peace. This is the first full-sized classical Chinese garden ever built outside China and it's quite an experience, even on a rain-soaked day. Most people don't know this, but check out the eaves on the garden roofs—they have been shaped to turn rain showers into beaded curtains of water. Repeat the mantra: I am a Wet Coaster…Ommmm. The Dr. Sun Yat-Sen Classical Chinese Garden is located at 578 Carall Street.

GREAT SPORTS BARS

By Jonathan McDonald

Sports bar rule number 1: Don't pick fights. There's tons of testosterone that flows in your average sports bar, and you're bound to get beaten up. Sports bar rule number 2: Be careful what you order. Some sports bars are more renowned for their food than others. Sports bar rule number 3: Feel free to show emotion. Fist-pumping is good. High-fives are fine. Even crying—if necessary—is perfectly acceptable. Study these well and you'll fit in like a regular in ten of the great sports bars around Vancouver and the Lower Mainland.

THE SHARK CLUB: This sports bar in Langley is a beauty. It can get crowded, but never feels crowded. That's because it's airy with high ceilings, a loft area and pool tables in the basement. You can't beat the noise level: There's no need to yell at your buddy over the music. You can watch a game in peace on any number of televisions over the bar and spread around the restaurant, including the small screens built into the wall around the cozy two-person booths. The Shark Club is located at 20169-88th Avenue in Langley.

LEGENDS: Legends is a great name for a sports bar. This Richmond bar is packed with the jerseys of hometown heroes. The Steveston Packers high school uniforms are up here. Ditto for the legendary lacrosse team, the Richmond Roadrunners, of which bar owner Glenn Jensen is a prominent alumnus. Small and intimate, Legends has the usual array of televisions and a big screen. Legends is located at 8220 Lansdowne Road in Richmond.

THE SHARK CLUB: This is the granddaddy of all sports bars in Vancouver. It's a block from GM Place and BC Place, which means it's packed before and after games. Great big TVs, plenty of fans hoping to catch a glimpse of the athletes after they've showered, this is best of the neighbourhood joints which include Courtnall's Sports Grill, Beatty Street Bar & Grill, and Dix. The Shark Club is located at 180 West Georgia. Courtnall's Sports Grill is located at 118 Robson Street. Beatty Street Bar & Grill is located at 773 Beatty Street. Dix Barbecue and Brewery is at 871 Beatty Street.

THE DOVER ARMS: There are few sports bars in this town that turn people away at the door at breakfast time, but that's been the case at the Dover Arms. Some people call it dumpy; we prefer to call it charming. Hockey takes a backseat to soccer. It's never too early to plan to go there for the latest European or World soccer tournament, since it will be rocking. The Dover Arms is located at 981 Denman Street.

MALONE'S: Looking for a good place to watch the Stanley Cup in the late months of spring? If your team is out of the play-offs and you couldn't care less, hit the patio and watch the beautiful people hit Kits Beach. During the week appetizers are half-price. Malone's is located at 2202 Cornwall Avenue.

JAKE & ELWOOD'S/MONTANA'S/QUEEN'S CROSS/ PEMBERTON STATION: After a nice game of golf on the North Shore, you don't have to go all that far to put your feet up and watch someone else in action. Of the North Vancouver and West Vancouver hangouts, the best would be Jake & Elwood's Sports Bar, located at 1080 Park Royal South,

West Vancouver. Other good bets in North Vancouver: Montana's at 135 West 1st, Queen's Cross Neighbourhood Pub at 2989 Lonsdale, and Pemberton Station at 135 Pemberton.

JIMY MAC'S PUB: Just a few blocks from Langley's Shark Club, Jimy Mac's Pub could very well be a world away. In the olde English Tudor style, Jimy Mac's is the kind of rugged place you can put your feet up on the table. Of course, it's possible you'd get smacked for it. The atrium is a nice bright room where you can get away from the noise, but where you really want to be is in the room that's got three big-screen televisions lined up in what could be the ideal sports viewing room. Jimy Mac's is located at 19935-96th Avenue, Langley.

JOHN B. NEIGHBOURHOOD PUB: Classy—that's how this pub has been described. Great seats, great sets, and the place really hops on a Thursday night. It also has a great fireplace for the ultimate in sports viewing pleasure. The John B. Neighbourhood Pub is located at 1000 Austin Street in Coquitlam.

CARLOS 'N BUD'S: Some people might disagree with this choice. Does it fit the mode of typical sports bar? Maybe not. But it's got one enormous television, is packed to the gills for the big events, and has some of the best service in town. Carlos 'n Bud's is located at 555 Pacific Street.

THE REEF/BREAKERS: Okay, there's two…and they're American, but these two sports bars in Point Roberts are excellent sources of American satellite television and those great American commercials. It's quieter at The Reef; if you're in the mood for a little more than sports, slip over to the adjoining Breakers. If you're lucky, you might even see owner Gene Kiniski, the great pro wrestler. The Reef and Breakers are located at 531 Marine Drive in Point Roberts.

GREAT CITIES IN THE LOWER MAINLAND

BY DAVID SPANER

You're tired of all the healthy, outdoorsy, recreational activities the Vancouver area has to offer and you just want a taste of a fat old big city. Luckily for you, Vancouver has a knack for looking like other places, which is one reason film producers like shooting here. Here are some of the places in the Lower Mainland that instantly suggest other cities.

LOS ANGELES: Kingsway. Just take a cruise down Kingsway and you've captured the feel of fast vehicles, fast food and fast-talking car dealers that's everywhere in L.A. Kingsway is L.A. without palm trees.

**SYDNEY, AUSTRALIA:** Canada Place. Head to the north end of Granville, look out to sea and suddenly you're contemplating Sydney's much-hyped waterfront opera house.

**MIAMI:** Villa Maris, 2222 Bellevue, West Vancouver. Stop at this address on the North Shore waterfront and you're face-to-face with a pink behemoth of an apartment building. This is Miami Beach at its kitschy 1950s' best (or worst).

**SEATTLE:** Starbucks. Some people in the rest of Canada connect Starbucks in particular and coffee in general with Vancouver, but walk into Starbucks, any Starbucks, and you're walking into Seattle.

**NEW YORK:** The Pacific Cinematheque. This theatre with its small lobby, unadorned walls and esoteric films is a Manhattan art-house cinema alive in downtown Vancouver. Pacific Cinematheque is located at 1131 Howe Street.

**SAN FRANCISCO:** The Lions Gate Bridge. Cross the Lions Gate and you could be headed for Sausalito instead of the North Shore. Both bridges were partially constructed at Burnaby's old Dominion Bridge site.

**MONTREAL:** Kaplan's Delicatessen. The booths and the rest of the interior of this Jewish deli at 41st and Oak is practically identical to the legendary Snowdon Deli in Montreal. Doesn't have the classic bagels but the look is eerily familiar.

**COPENHAGEN, DENMARK:** Girl in Wetsuit statue. Take a spin around Stanley Park until you arrive at Vancouver's version of Copenhagen's Little Mermaid statue. Instead of the original's fins, this one has legs, like the Aqua men and women that live in this city—people so accustomed to rain they've formed a part-human, part-amphibian species unique to the Lower Mainland.

TORONTO: Tim Horton's Donuts. Toronto loves its 24-hour donuterias and Horton played for the Maple Leafs, so just order a sugary chocolate number and imagine you're in the Big Smoke. You can find a Tim Horton's in North Vancouver at Marine Drive and Philip Avenue.

METROPOLIS: Sun Tower. There was a time when the building at Beatty and Pender housed a newspaper and was topped by a neon sun. It looked so much like the *Daily Planet* building that children would look to it in hopes of seeing Superman fly off. The Metropolis Sun Tower is located on the southeastern corner of Pender Street and Beatty Street.

GREAT SUMMER FESTIVALS

By Stuart Derdeyn

Around here, we don't wait for the official June 21 arrival of summer to get busy getting down. From mid-May to late September, the parties run full-bore. There are almost too many to choose from. Not a week goes by in the month of July that doesn't feature an organised happening worth checking out. So many events get packed into such a short period of time that by Labour Day a condition some dub "fest-fatigue" sets in. A combination of sleep and bank account deprivation, fest-fatigue still doesn't stop us. In fact, until the last light of late summer fades away to grey and we head into the fall, and indoors, British Columbians celebrate the light. Here are the ten best festivals of the summer season, all within a day's drive of Vancouver.

VANCOUVER INTERNATIONAL CHILDREN'S FESTIVAL: Silly adult, this is for kids. Even so, it's not unusual to see parents pushing to the front rows at shows such as Fred Penner, Charlotte Diamond and Heather Bishop, allegedly to get their tiny ones better seats. The pan-global programming of this annual "tot-stock" means the entertainment is as likely to mesmerise adults as it is the intended audience. The Vancouver International Children's Festival takes place each year at Vanier Park (behind the Pacific Space Centre). For information, call 708-5655.

VANCOUVER INTERNATIONAL DRAGON BOAT FESTIVAL: The ancient Chinese sport of dragon boating has caught on here like fire from the mythical creature's mouth. Once the big drums go boom, the paddles hit the water and the races begin. And if you get bored watching the boats, there are the concerts, dances and food fairs on-site to enjoy. The Vancouver International Dragon Boat Festival takes place at the Plaza of Nations, Concord Pacific Place and on the waters of False Creek. Call 688-2382 for more information.

DUMAURIER INTERNATIONAL JAZZ FESTIVAL VANCOUVER: As many acts as there are answers to "What is jazz?" make this a signature musical showcase. Everyone from the serious be-boppers to jazz newcomers can enjoy any one of the 400 or so concerts around town. The 10-day run is bookended by two weekends of free gigs in Gastown and at the Roundhouse at the corner of Pacific and Davie. The DuMaurier International Jazz Festival Vancouver takes place at various venues throughout the Lower Mainland. For information call 872-5200.

HARRISON FESTIVAL OF THE ARTS: For over 20 years, this resort town at the top of the valley has hosted an eclectic mix of family, folk, First Nations and African artists. The setting is one of the most beautiful in the whole province. For an extra treat, relax after a long day of festing with a soak in the public hot springs in the centre of town. The Harrison Festival of the Arts takes place at Harrison Hot Springs. Call 681-2771 or 604-796-3664 for tickets and information.

MERRITT MOUNTAIN MUSIC FESTIVAL: Calling all cowboys and cowgirls, Nashville's biggest stars appear in British Columbia's biggest hoedown. Past featured stars have included Dwight Yokum, Kenny Rogers, Diamond Rio and Deana Carter. Be sure to pack plenty of water and sunscreen. The site location is renowned for its dust and heat. The

Merritt Mountain Music Festival takes place at the Merritt Fairgrounds. Call 525-3300 for information, 250-860-5989 for tickets.

VANCOUVER FOLK MUSIC FESTIVAL: As if listening to amazing tunes from distant lands or discovering local troubadours on one of six stages isn't enough, how about hanging out in one of the city's best parks, gazing over Burrard Inlet at the North Shore mountains and watching the sunset? You've entered the Folk zone, and for one weekend each year, there is no place like it in Vancouver. The Vancouver Folk Music Festival takes place at Jericho Beach Park. Call 1-800-883-FOLK for more information.

MISSION FOLK MUSIC FESTIVAL: Now in its second decade, the Mission gathering is a key stop for Canadian artists. This is your chance to scout out the up and coming talents on the Canadian folk music scene. The equally beautiful setting boasts camping spots—a real bonus for tired folkies. The Mission Folk Festival takes place at River Heritage Park. Call 604-904-5657 for information and tickets.

ABBOTSFORD INTERNATIONAL AIRSHOW: Besides the usual contingent of contemporary military hardware, there's plenty of flying firepower of years gone by at this airshow. Air aficionados from around the globe flock to this airshow where some of the finest pilots around put planes through their paces. The Abbotsford International Airshow takes place at Abbotsford Airport. Call 604-280-4444 for tickets and information.

ILLUMINAIRES FESTIVAL OF LIGHTS LANTERN PROCESSION: This festival is one of the signature family evenings in the city. Fire dancers, crazed brass bands, costumed kayakers and lanterns burning everywhere makes this night walk around the lake unlike any other. Come prepared for a truly mystical and magical evening. The Illuminaires Festival of Lights Lantern Procession takes place at Trout Lake Park and Community Centre (3550 Victoria Street) at dusk. Admission is by donation.

UNDER THE VOLCANO: Celebrating over a decade of promoting political activism and community organising, this event isn't preachy or precious. Under the Volcano is an explosion of fun. It's the only place where you'll see pierced punks, Raging Grannies and everyone else dancing together to an eclectic array of musicians. This festival is worth it for people-watching value alone. The Under the Volcano Festival takes place in North Vancouver at Cate's Park, near Deep Cover. Admission is by donation.

GREAT THINGS TO DO ON CANADA DAY

By Glen Schaefer

Still hanging together at over 130 years old, the land of maple syrup, cheap dollars, back bacon and Burton Cummings keeps rolling along. Canadians don't get the high-octane patriotic juice out of our national holiday that the Americans do three days later, and there may never be an action movie called Canada Day. But our day is a still a great day to celebrate the different charms of this spectacular land. We rounded up a list of ten suggestions but as with the national anthem, fill free to improvise.

GET UNDER THE SAILS: At Canada Place, the classic Canada Day experience annually pulls in a crowd of about 100,000. Events include citizenship swearing-in and over 70 free performances. Pick up free ticket vouchers for the head-line evening show early, though, to avoid disappointment. Stick around for the spectacular harbour fireworks after the show. Call 666-8477 for more information.

GET SOME HARBOUR AIR: From outside Canada Place, there are harbour cruises on the half-hour from the cruise ship level. You can tour a patrol frigate, watch a tugboat ballet and fireboat demonstrations. Or you can relax and watch the sailboats and cruise ships go by.

GET ALPINE: Cypress Mountain in West Vancouver has an annual free pancake breakfast, free tubing, sledding and tobogganing. Or try the Grouse Grind in North Vancouver on Canada Day. At the top of Grouse are snowboard demonstrations, logger sports shows and free music from local groups. Grinders who bring non-perishable food items or monetary donations to the Food Bank get a free Skyride down the mountain.

GET TO KNOW YOUR NEIGHBOURS: Even if you're just visiting our fair city, most city and municipal recreation departments have something going on. Surrey's Bear Creak Park hosts an annual daylong pancake breakfast, BC Lions meet-and-greets, music and crafts. Burnaby Village Museum has a variety show and serves up a giant flag cake with strawberries and butter-cream icing. Fort Langley has live entertainment in the village centre.

GET TO KNOW THE NATIONAL ANTHEM: Can you sing our national anthem in both official languages? Prepare for the Canada Day celebrations by learning more about the history and traditions of our wonderful country. The Vancouver Public Library at 350 West Georgia Street is always a good place to start your research. Just remember that it will be closed on the July 1st holiday, as will most businesses.

GET JAZZY: The Vancouver Jazz Festival presents free concerts on Canada Day on Granville Island, noon to midnight. Combine that with a bit of browsing through the markets and walkways in this oasis of colour. Take advantage of the free False Creek Ferry and Aquabus rides for anyone dressed head-to-toe in red and white. Other musically inclined folks might prefer the Stardust Picnic at the Plaza of Nations.

GET FISHY: The Salmon Festival on and around Steveston docks has a trade show, rides and a craft fair. There are also fishing-related contests. The parade starts at 8:30 a.m., and the salmon barbecue is not to be missed. The Steveston Hotel is always packed, and traditionally, a pack of burly bikers rides through the bar—in one door and out the other.

GET HISTORICAL: Port Moody, site of the original western terminus of the Canadian Pacific Railway, has Golden Spike Days starting at 10 a.m. with people in period costumes, paddlewheeler rides and historical displays. At 10:15 p.m, the Port Moody fire fighters set off a fireworks show from a barge. Events take place at the Port Moody Station Museum at 2734 Murray Street and on the waterfront.

BE A COUCH POTATO: CBC-TV's Canada Day gala is annually presented from Parliament Hill in Ottawa, Canada's capital city. The broadcast includes a mighty wad of bubble-gum rockers from the 1960s and '70s. For those of you looking for a Canada Day trip down memory lane, this is the event for you.

HAVE A CANADA DAY PICNIC WITH YOUR FAMILY AND FRIENDS: Second Beach in Stanley Park is a highly recommended picnic spot. It's got a playground, swimming pool, beach, and lots of grass. If you have more lofty ambitions, drive up to Whistler and take a gondola to the top for a snow picnic.

GREAT THINGS TO DO WITH KIDS THIS SUMMER

By Hardip Johal

There's no doubt about it; Vancouver is a kid-friendly town. Whether you're here for a week or live here permanently, there's no shortage of things to do with your children. Each one of these suggestions is guaranteed to stop the inevitable summer plague of "I'm bored…there's nothing to do." Have fun!

UNIVERSITY OF BRITISH COLUMBIA'S MUSEUM OF ANTHROPOLOGY: There's a lot here for the kids to explore, including two Haida Houses and the museum's "visible storage" area, where they'll find 15,000 objects from around the world—including games and toys from other countries. This vast collection from different cultures is kept in drawers, which kids will love opening to see what's inside. The Museum of Anthropology is located at 6393 NW Marine Drive (UBC grounds), Vancouver. Phone 822-5087 for hours and admission rates.

A DAY ON THE SUNSHINE COAST: A 40-minute ride aboard a BC Ferry will take you from Horseshoe Bay to Langdale on the Sunshine Coast. Ten minutes away from Langdale, you'll find Gibsons, home of the Elphinstone Pioneer Museum, Molly's Reach Restaurant (the original set for the TV series *The Beachcombers*) and a seawall. About half an hour away, Pender Harbour features fishing and hiking. For more information call Vancouver Tourism at 739-0823 or 1-800-667-3306 outside Greater Vancouver.

VANCOUVER MARITIME MUSEUM/ST. ROCH NATIONAL HISTORIC SITE: The highlight here is the *St. Roch*. Built in 1928 for the Royal Canadian Mounted Police, the ship was used as a patrol and supply ship in the western Arctic for more than 20 years. Visitors are welcome to go aboard and explore the ship. The Vancouver Maritime Museum is located at 1905 Ogden Avenue in Vancouver. Phone 257-8300 for hours and rates.

WEST COAST RAILWAY HERITAGE PARK: A must for locomotive-loving kids and their parents, this 48,564-square-metre (12-acre) riverside park includes cabooses, steam, diesel and electric locomotives. When those little legs get tired, hop aboard the miniature train ride that takes visitors from one end of the park to the other. Pack a lunch and make a day of it. The West Coast Railway Heritage Park is located at 39645 Government Road in Squamish. (From Highway 99, turn west at Industrial Way and follow signs to the park.) Phone 604-898-9336 for hours and rates.

LOWER SEYMOUR CONSERVATION RESERVE: Who says nothing's free? It doesn't cost anything to enjoy this living forest. There's even a 10-kilometre (approximately 6-mile) paved road for inline skating, riding your bike or walking.

The paved road leads to a 1.7-kilometre (1-mile) boardwalk trail through old-growth forest. Fishing is available at Rice Lake. The Lower Seymour Conservation Reserve is located off Exit 22 on Highway 1 in North Vancouver. Follow Lillooet Road right through to the Rice Lake parking lot. Phone 604-987-1273 for more information.

BURNABY HERITAGE VILLAGE MUSEUM: Take the children back in time to this re-creation of a turn-of-the-century village. Mingle with costumed townsfolk as you explore the 40,470-square-metre (10-acre) site, which includes period homes, a one-room schoolhouse, and blacksmith demonstrations. Pick the steed or carriage of your choice on the vintage carousel. The Burnaby Heritage Village Museum is located at 6501 Deer Lake Avenue in Burnaby (Exit 33 off Highway 1). Phone 293-6501 for hours and rates.

PACIFIC SPACE CENTRE: Explore the final frontiers—space and time—on two new Virtual Voyages Simulator rides: Comet Impact blasts off to intercept a comet before it strikes earth; Dinosaur Simulator takes you back in time to see, hear and feel what it was like to be a dinosaur. The Pacific Space Centre is located at 1100 Chestnut Street in Vancouver. Phone 738-7827 for hours and rates.

CAPILANO SUSPENSION BRIDGE AND PARK: Cross the world's longest pedestrian suspension bridge (137 metres; 449 feet). Seventy metres (230 feet) below the swinging bridge are the rushing waters of Capilano River. Pack a picnic lunch and make a day of it in the park, which features nature trails, waterfalls, ponds and old-growth evergreens. You can also watch First Nations carvers work on totem poles, masks and bowls. The Capilano Suspension Bridge and Park is located at 3735 Capilano Road in North Vancouver. Phone 985-7474 for admission rates.

FORT LANGLEY NATIONAL HISTORIC SITE: Costumed guides use stories, re-enactments and demonstrations to bring this restored Hudson's Bay trading post to life. Built in 1827, Fort Langley is home to the oldest building on

BC's mainland. Visitors can pan for gold, watch a blacksmith working at his forge and view weaving demonstrations. Plan for a 60- to 90-minute visit. Fort Langley National Historical Site is located at 23433 Mavis Avenue in Fort Langley (50 kilometres or 30 miles east of Vancouver). Phone 604-513-4777 for hours and admission rates.

SHAKESPEARE UNDER THE STARS: To expose the kids to the theatre without exposing your wallet, check out Shakespeare Under the Stars at Granville Island in August (Monday to Saturday evenings at 8 p.m.). Admission is free for all. Bring a family blanket to cuddle under while you and the kids take the works of the Bard at the Performance Works Outdoor Stage. Phone 875-3350 for information.

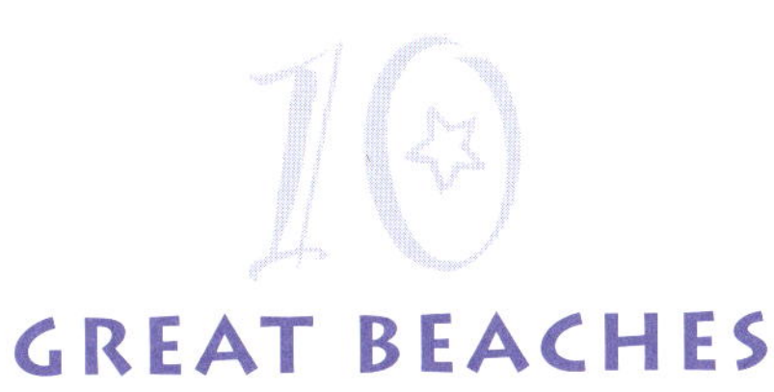

GREAT BEACHES

GLEN SCHAEFER

Ah...summer. The word is practically synonymous with "beach." Rows of bodies glistening in the sun, long-legged girls and bare-shouldered boys spilling out of open-topped Jeeps at beach-side, their zinc-smudged noses following the breeze off the water, children shrieking with joy as they play in the water. Yes, life certainly is a beach.

Surrounded by the Pacific Ocean and a plethora of lakes inland, Vancouver and the Lower Mainland certainly don't suffer from a shortage of beaches. Here are ten great beaches, all highly recommended by *Province* readers, and all within a few hour's drive of Vancouver.

WHITE PINE BEACH, SASAMAT LAKE: Situated in Belcarra Regional Park, this gem is a little out of the way for almost everyone but worth it. There are no crabs, no seaweed and the fresh water is warmer than the ocean. In addition, the gradual drop-off makes it a very kid-friendly beach. Ringed by dense woods and cradled between shaggy hills north-west of Port Moody, the lake is an antidote for all things urban. If it weren't for the all-ages crowd on the beach, you'd forget you were anywhere near the city.

BUNTZEN LAKE: A short drive north-east from Sasamat Lake is Buntzen Lake, actually a BC Hydro reservoir. This beach is a bit higher, a bit cooler, with fishing and canoe rentals also on offer. Trivia note: Horror-movie fans will recognise Buntzen's charms in the locally filmed giant alligator movie *Lake Placid* starring Bridget Fonda and Bill Pullman. To get to Sasamet Lake or Buntzen Lake, head north on Ioco Road (east of Port Moody). The road eventually winds westward and you'll hang a right on First Avenue. Then follow the signs. And come early on hot days to beat the parking-lot rush.

SPANISH BANKS: This is the kind of beach where the worries just fall away from your shoulders on a sunny, low-tide day and you can run, walk or boogie-board for what seems like forever. Barbecue dinner as the sun goes down, rest on the grass and see the kids' kites trade space on the horizon with the distant sailboats. Watch a dozen balls bouncing lazily in the distance over as many beach volleyball courts. Spanish Banks Beach is located along NW Marine Drive in Vancouver.

WHITE ROCK: Another low-tide wonder, this stretch of south-facing sand is among the best in the world for castle building. It was a sad day a few years back when the beach's annual sand-castle-building contest was cancelled because it got too big for the town. Up on Marine Drive, there's a little bit of mobile California ambience, as what seems like every convertible in the Lower Mainland trolls past the T-shirt shops and burger places. Beach Boys songs were made for this. White Rock Beach is located along Marine Drive in Surrey.

JERICHO BEACH: This is the beach for those looking for a great place to lay in the sun without having to worry about rubbing elbows with your beach-blanket neighbour. Another perk, the trails through the nearby wooded, marshy park are a shady way to walk a bit of the heat off. Jericho Beach is located along 4th Avenue in Vancouver.

ENGLISH BAY: The classic urban beach. High-rise apartments and Denman Street behind you as you lie back on the sand. Inline skaters whiz past your head. Strap on your own headphones, lie back and sonically cocoon yourself against the city blur—everyone else does. Those with kids might want to head along the sea wall to the pool-waterpark to the west at Second Beach.

AMBLESIDE BEACH: West Vancouver's entry makes its mark as the sandy front-row seat to watch the cruise ships slip gracefully out from under Lions Gate Bridge. The North Shore's western end also misses a lot of the rain and clouds that bounce off the mountains and spill on parts east.

WRECK BEACH: For those who truly want to get in touch with nature. When it's good, the Lower Mainland's official clothing-optional beach is great. This isn't the body-beautiful beach, it's the body-somewhat-lumpy-but-I'm-OK-with-that beach. Wreck Beach is located in the University Endowment Lands off NW Marine Drive.

KITS BEACH: This is Vancouver's unofficial singles beach. Looking—and the eye contact, body-language thing that goes with it—comes with the territory. Trash talk on the basketball court wafts over and blends with boom-box rock 'n' roll, dipped in coconut suntan oil. Sunscreen is a foreign term here. You'd swear you were in a *Baywatch* episode. Kits Beach is located off of Cornwall Avenue in Vancouver.

CULTUS LAKE: The heat of the Fraser Valley needs an escape valve and this is it. Plan to spend most of the day in the water, with most of the people of Chilliwack and Abbotsford alongside you, when the scorching weather really kicks in. This is a mecca for water-skiing and jet-skiing. Cultus Lake is located just prior to Chilliwack off of Highway 99.

GREAT POOLS

Stuart Derdeyn and Jonathan McDonald

Beaches are great, but some days you want to slip into a body of water that's temperature-regulated. And clean. And clear. Hey, there aren't any rules that say you have to get your summer dose of aquatic fun in the ocean. For all of the fabulous beaches in the Lower Mainland, there are an equal number of pools. To maximise your enjoyment, be sure to follow the rules set out by each aquatic facility. Here are ten great places to get wet around here.

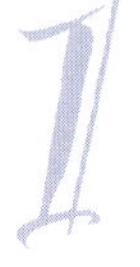

SECOND BEACH: This is the finest of the city's outdoor pools. It's open every summer until Labour Day and it's considered by many to be the best post-Seawall jog cool down around. Even if you aren't a jogger, swimming in this pool by the ocean brings to mind Mediterranean splendour on blinding hot summer days. Second Beach is located in Stanley Park. For hours and admission rates, call 257-8371.

KITS BEACH: "At 137.5 metres long, this is the triathlete's pool," says cashier Rebecca Ford. "Almost everybody who swims here works out hard." Even if you're not a super-athlete, you can feel virtuous as you do a few arm-killing laps in this outdoor pool. Afterwards relax and watch the sailboats and wind-surfers against the backdrop of the North Shore mountains. Kits Beach Pool is located at Yew and Cornwall. Call 731-0011 for hours and admission rates.

WATERMANIA AQUATIC CENTRE: It's okay to be inside on a sunny day when there's this much wonderful water. Three-storey water slides, a wave pool that churns out waves suitable for Big Kahunas everywhere, and a multi-laned 50-metre competition-size pool that's perfect for length swimming are a few of the perks of this indoor shrine to aquatic fun. The Watermania Aquatic Centre is located at 12300 Entertainment Boulevard in Richmond. For hours and admission rates, call 448-5353.

SURREY SPORTS AND LEISURE COMPLEX: This is one of the Lower Mainland's newest aquatic facilities. Aside from water slides, saunas and steam rooms, the complex's 50-metre competition pool has a moveable floor. The shallow end can be altered from standard depth to a zero-entry angle for special programs for seniors, children and persons with disabilities. The Surrey Sports and Leisure Complex is located on Fraser Highway, between 164th and 168th streets. For hours and admission rates, call 543-0300.

EILEEN DAILLY LEISURE POOL AND FITNESS CENTRE: This Burnaby pool doesn't appear to be any different than most aquatic centres. But when the sprinkler system pumps up the fun in the shallow end on occasion, watch out for the fun. This pool also boasts some of the best Tarzan ropes in town. Just make sure that the person ahead of you has swam out of the way before you do your best ape-call. The Eileen Dailly Leisure Pool and Fitness Centre is located at 240 Willingdon Road in Burnaby. Call 298-7946 for hours and admission rates.

HIGH CREEK RECREATION CENTRE: This small indoor centre got a multi-million dollar face lift, adding racquetball and squash courts, as well as a pro-shop. It's the smaller size and family friendliness that finds folks heading here instead of one of the bigger busier Coquitlam Pools. High Creek

Recreation Centre is located at 1379 Laurier, Port Coquitlam. For hours and admission rates, call 927-7946.

CANADA GAMES POOL & FITNESS CENTRE: This fully loaded Olympic facility is New Westminster's only indoor swimming area. Try out your fastest front-crawl in the 100-metre pool. Test your skills on the 10-metre diving platform. Then close your eyes and imagine yourself receiving the gold medal. The Canada Games Pool & Fitness Centre is located at 65 East 6th Avenue, New Westminster. Call 526-4281 for hours and admission rates.

MAPLE RIDGE LEISURE CENTRE: What sets this facility apart is the attention it pays to the little people. "We really pay attention to the kids here. It's very family-friendly," says supervisor Trish Wood. There's even a separate sauna area for youths at this original prototype for the rest of the Lower Mainland's indoor leisure centres. Maple Ridge Leisure Centre is located at 11925 Haney Place. Call 467-7322 for hours and admission rates.

VANCOUVER AQUATIC CENTRE: When it rains, city swimmers pour into this indoor space. Many of Vancouver's competitive swim clubs call the Centre home. You can also see some great water polo action here as well. The fast lane lives up to its designation, so judge your speed against the swimmers already in there. There's nothing worse than feeling like the slowest swimmer in the pool. The Vancouver Aquatic Centre is located at 1050 Beach Avenue. For hours and rates, call 665-3424.

SPLASHDOWN: Technically, this isn't a swimming pool. But only technically. The centrepiece of this outdoor jewel en route to the Tsawwassen ferry terminal is a smallish, usually uninhabited pool that wild-eye fun-seekers flee after crashing into it from the River Run. What is the River Run, you ask? A go-for-broke, douse-your-neighbours plunge in tubes. Splashdown features a half-dozen slides of varying difficulties. Splashdown is located at 4799 North Lelum Way in Tsawwassen. For hours and admission rates, call 943-2251.

GREAT CAMPSITES

BY HARDIP JOHAL

Vancouver's one of the "greenest" cities in the world. Nestled between ocean and mountains, it's hard to get any closer to nature than this. But if your ideal vacation includes campfires and s'mores, here are ten great campsites to appease your woodsy soul. All locations are located within a day's drive of Vancouver. Just remember the golden rule of camping: you bring out what you take in.

CATHEDRAL: Richmond's Jean Dutton says getting to Cathedral Provincial Park isn't exactly a snap, but the stunning vistas are well worth the effort. "It feels as if you're on top of the world because you're about nine thousand feet above sea level," says Dutton. Bounded on the south by the Washington–B.C. border and on the north by the Ashnola River, the 33,000-hectare (127-square-mile) park—about 30 kilometres (approximately 19 miles) south-west of Keremeos in the Okanagan Mountain Range—is home to mule deer, mountain goat and bighorn sheep. Another attraction is the soaring rock formations, the best known of which are Smokey the Bear and Giant Cleft.

EMORY CREEK: This private campsite 18 kilometres (approximately 11 miles) north of Hope garners rave reviews from Vancouverites and tourists alike. Well-manicured campsites are nestled under a canopy of towering fir, cedar, alder, maple and birch trees. An extra perk for those not so enthusiastic about the whole camping experience: the outhouses are complete with flush toilets and fresh flower bouquets. Emory Creek also offers fishing, bear and sturgeon sightings.

LAC LE JEUNE: Le Jeune Provincial Park, 37 kilometres (approximately 23 miles) south-west of Kamloops, has thrilled campers and anglers for years. It offers the plaintive cries of loons waking you for breakfast, a sandy, sun-baked beach and the most spectacular lightning storms in BC. (The advantage of this is that your wife or companion will cuddle you even longer at night.) Most of all, it gives you spectacular trout fishing all year round.

SASQUATCH: Scout leader Jim Brown is a fan of Hick's Lake in Sasquatch Provincial Park, 6 kilometres (approximately 4 miles) north of Harrison Hot Springs. "It's far enough away from civilization yet not so far away as to be nearly inaccessible," says the Burnaby resident. "The lake is beautiful and—if one doesn't mind the chilly temperatures—good for swimming." Other attractions include shoreline fishing and trails suitable for beginning hikers.

CEDAR GROVE: Burnaby's Vicky Robinson raves about the private Cedar Grove Tent and Trailer Park on Vancouver Island. "The campground has all the amenities—showers, laundry, playground, tables, firepits and a river for swimming," she says. "It's also centrally located so you can make many day trips around the island. Next door is a waterslide and two blocks away is Qualicum Beach, with warm, shallow water and the tide way out a good part of the day."

NEWCASTLE ISLAND: North Vancouver's Kimberly Dolmage recommends this park near Nanaimo. "It's a wonderful place to go because there is excellent hiking, nice beaches, caves that you can explore and large fields to play on," she says.

"The wildlife is abundant. There are deer, raccoons, rabbits, many different birds and even a few garter snakes."

KOA CAMPGROUND, SALMON ARM: KOA campgrounds are a chain of campsites across the United States and Canada. The campsites are always clean and well looked after. Some offer showers and firewood. The KOA Campground in Salmon Arm offers the added perks of a pool and a games room and the opportunity to meet fellow campers from all over North America. Reservations are accepted for all KOA campsites.

ALICE LAKE: Swimming, canoeing, kayaking and a 6-kilometre (almost 4-mile) trail that takes hikers and cyclists past four lakes beckon campers to Alice Lake Provincial Park, about 13 kilometres (approximately 8 miles) north of Squamish. Amenities include cold water taps throughout the 396-hectare (980-acre) park, hot-water showers and guided walks. Campsite reservations are accepted for some of the 108 campsites, while others are first-come, first-served.

BIG BAR: Maple Ridge resident Mike Williams, who's visited 95 per cent of BC's provincial parks, recommends Big Bar Provincial Park. "Camping near the water is one of the nicest parts," says Williams, who has parked his trailer on the shores of Big Bar Lake six times. "The fishing's really good; there's really nice rainbow trout. Whatever I catch, we cook it right there and eat it." Big Bar is 42 kilometres (approximately 26 miles) north-west of Clinton off Highway 97. A 34-kilometre (approximately 21-mile) gravel road takes you to the park.

WILDWOOD RESORT: Port Coquitlam's Shelley Trellert is wild about Wildwood Resort on the shores of Whatcom Lake in Washington. "You camp on grass, which means your kids can stay really clean," says Trellert. "There's a nice playground and logged-in areas where the kids can swim without going out too far—and the water's warm. It's also a great water-skiing lake." Take the I-5 to the Lakeway Exit—25 minutes past Bellis Fair—and it's a private site so don't forget to make a reservation first.

CAMPING TIPS:

Before heading out with your camping gear, call ahead and make a reservation.

That said, not all provincial park campgrounds take reservations. For information on provincial park fees and reservation availability, try the provincial parks website at www.env.gov.bc.ca. To make a reservation in a provincial park, call Discover Camping at 689-9025 from Greater Vancouver or 1-800-689-9025. For more information on a provincial park, call whichever number below corresponds to the area you wish to visit. (The BC Ministry of Environment, Lands and Parks is listed in the blue pages of the phone book.)

Lower Mainland District 924-2200

South Vancouver Island 250-391-2300

Strathcona District 250-954-4600

Okanagan District 250-494-6500

Thompson River District 250-851-3000

Cariboo District 250-398-4414

GREAT PLACES TO WALK YOUR DOG

By Dana Gee

You may have noticed that Vancouver is a very dog-friendly city. A stroll down any street will reveal mutts mingling with purebreds in carefree abandon. In such an urban city, it may seem difficult to find a place that both you and your dog will agree on for a daily walk. There are actually a number of great places to enjoy the outdoors with your dog. Here are ten of the best.

MUNDY PARK: Local morning news anchor Lynn Collier's dogs Donovan, Lucas and Monty (Irish Wolfhound, miniature Schnauzer and Shepherd cross, respectively) give this spot a resounding paws up. What makes this park a big hit with Collier's pack is it's a leash-free zone before 10 a.m. and after 5 p.m. "They love to romp in the park and meet up with their friends," says Collier. "There are doggie bags available at every park entrance, which is very important." Mundy Park is located in Coquitlam.

FRASER RIVER DIKE IN RICHMOND: The dike, with its spectacular bird-rich river views, is a walker's dream. Says one *Province* staff reporter: "It's really pleasant for the dogs and it's pleasant for the owners." If you enter at the foot of Blundell Road, you'll find washrooms and doggie-doo bags.

DERBY REACH PROVINCIAL PARK: "We are a family of three—myself, my daughter Mireya and our Border Collie cross Mike," says Nora Hooper of Aldergrove. "Our sunny-day favourite is Derby Reach. They have a semi-fenced, off-leash area that allows dogs and their friends beach access. On any day there is a bunch of dogs swimming or sharing a throw toy. My daughter likes to dig in the sand, and since this is a clean-up park she can do so." Derby Reach Provincial Park is located near Fort Langley. Fort Langley is east of Vancouver on Highway 1.

ALDERGROVE LAKE PARK: This park has several trails (some off-leash) with varying terrain. There's also a big field, perfect for a rousing game of fetch or Frisbee. You're in horse country here, so be careful and watch your dog. Aldergrove Lake Park is located at 8th Avenue and 272nd Street in Aldergrove.

DELTA NATURE RESERVE IN BURNS BOG: This area is a favourite among canine connoisseurs. There are lots of wooded areas to explore, a stream to swim in and even some muddy places to get into. The best thing about this walk is that dogs can go off leash and there aren't any vehicles to worry about. Delta Nature Reserve in Burns Bog is located at 72nd Avenue at Westview Drive in North Delta.

BATEMAN PARK: This park has everything a dog wants in an exercise location. There are off-leash areas, plenty of paths and a creek to swim in or get a quick drink. "All the dogs that go there seem to be very socialised, it is very nice," says Abbotsford's Randy Rast. Bateman Park is located off Bateman Road in Abbotsford.

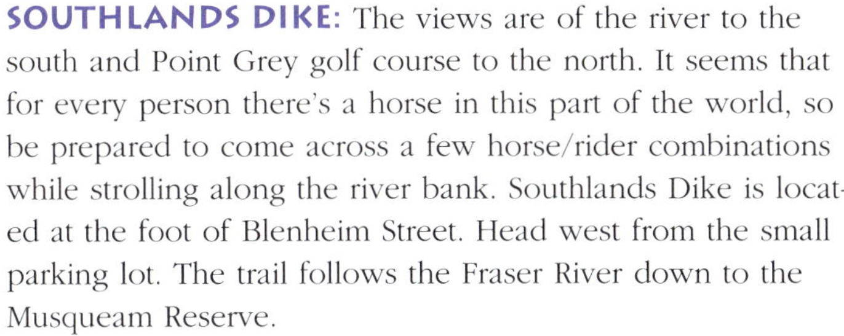

SOUTHLANDS DIKE: The views are of the river to the south and Point Grey golf course to the north. It seems that for every person there's a horse in this part of the world, so be prepared to come across a few horse/rider combinations while strolling along the river bank. Southlands Dike is located at the foot of Blenheim Street. Head west from the small parking lot. The trail follows the Fraser River down to the Musqueam Reserve.

BRIDGMAN PARK: This dog-friendly area offers a nice space to walk your dog with plenty of other dogs for spirited socialising. Nearby Lynn Creek is the perfect place for a quick dip and drink after a serious play session. Bridgman Park is located off Keith Road and Mountain Highway in North Vancouver.

PACIFIC SPIRIT PARK: For a truly woodsy dog walk, enter the wooded west-side trails of Pacific Spirit Park off of 16th Avenue. These oxygen-thick paths can be enjoyed for 20 minutes or two hours. Check out the Swordfern Trail; it's a beauty. A word of warning: mountain bikers can pop up at any time so keep your eyes open.

MARITIME MUSEUM AREA (BEACH JUST WEST OF MUSEUM ON KITS POINT): There's not a lot of space for any distance walking, so get your exercise first with a stroll along Kits Beach and through Vanier Park. Finish the outing back by letting your buddy bounce around at the off-leash beach.

GREAT COFFEE PLACES

By David Spaner

We live in a place that takes its coffee seriously. It has seeped into our consciousness, waking us up on the morning, keeping us up at night. In Vancouver, you're as likely to see someone walking down the street holding a coffee cup as an umbrella.

What is the difference between Vancouver and other cities in Canada? People talk about coffee here ("Where do you get yours?") the way they talk about bagels in Montreal and all-night donut stores in Toronto. We've compiled a list of ten great coffee places to start you on your tour of coffee in Vancouver and help you see what the buzz is all about.

TORREFAZIONE ITALIA CAFFE: This is one of a trio of excellent watering holes on the West 41st block of Kerrisdale, but this list is limited to one coffee place from any neighbourhood and Torrefazione gets high marks for all three criteria for inclusion: coffee, food and atmosphere. It has great, authentic Italian coffee, tasty treats brought in from a variety of bakeries, and a wonderful ambience with huge, comfortable chairs and beautiful mugs. Torrefazione is located at 2154 West 41st Avenue.

 **BEAN AROUND THE WORLD:** This coffeehouse remains among the best in the city. It grinds its own great coffee and has its own bakery. It also boasts seating out back and two rustic rooms with an eclectic assortment of chairs and tables, an Old West-style bar with a street view, a community bulletin board and piles of newspapers. Its collection of young baristas provides a glimpse at the latest alternative look. Bean Around the World is located at 1522 Marine Drive, West Vancouver.

 **CAFFE BELLA NAPOLI:** There are several spots on Commercial Drive that could make this list, from Café Calabria to Joe's, but the selection is Napoli. Right in the heart of Commercial Drive, it's a popular spot to watch Italian sports on television while drinking Italian coffee. It's one of those places that's only eight years old but has a been-here-forever look. It's definitely not the place to order low fat anything (although it's available). It's clean and bright with beautiful wall art, fine coffee and rich treats, including an acclaimed chocolate caramel hazelnut torte. Caffe Bella Napoli is located at 1670 Commercial Drive.

J.J. BEAN—THE COFFEE ROASTER (GRANVILLE ISLAND): This place is so unadorned that many customers don't even know its name, just referring to it as "the place at the entrance to Granville Island Market." There is no food here and the atmosphere consists of a functional service counter, but the coffee is so good and the baristas are so nice that customers keep coming back. J.J. Bean is located at the entrance to Granville Island Market.

 **BELLE'S COUNTRY MARKET:** From the outside, this looks pretty much like what it was: just a country store. Inside, however, grocery shelves share space with tables filled with morning customers drinking tasty coffee and devouring delicious homemade muffins and scones. This little oasis in Surrey also offers light lunches such as couscous and pasta salad. We recommend the crazy mandarin scone. Belle's Country Market is located at 3208-140th Street, Surrey.

THE STREAM: This coffee place is in a spectacular location on the north side of False Creek's seawall. For the price of a cup of coffee, you get a view of Granville Island, a marina, and the underbelly of the Burrard Bridge. There's comfortable indoor and outdoor seating, and the food and coffee's good, too. Morning brings in-house muffins, scones and carrot cake. There are also breakfast items such as cereal and omelettes. The Stream is located at 1012 Beach Avenue.

LAZY BAY CAFÉ & BAKERY: If you take a Sunday drive to Deep Cove, take a left at Mount Seymour Parkway and you'll find the Lazy Bay Café at Parkgate Village. The best thing about it is the setting in the middle of mountain greenery. The café has a spacious interior and it utilises an adjacent public plaza for outdoor seating. The coffee is okay, but Lazy Bay offers homemade jam and antipasto, light lunches and baked goods, such as a crunchy rustica roll with sundried tomatoes, herbs and Fontina cheese. The Lazy Bay Café & Bakery is located at 110-1151 Mount Seymour Road, North Vancouver.

WHITBY'S BOOKSTORE AND COFFEE HOUSE: A bookstore that serves coffee conjures romantic cinematic images of small shops in New England college towns. This one, however, has an ocean view in White Rock. The store has a counterculture sensibility with a cross-section of books on sexuality and spirituality. Inside, there's a fountain and large tables where customers can read or write for hours. There's also outside seating where coffee drinkers can watch the sea. The food and house-blend coffee is all right, but what really gives Whitby's its top marks is the ambience. Whitby's is located at 14837 Marine Drive, White Rock.

BOJANGLES: Robert De Niro isn't the only performer who has a Vancouver restaurant named after him. There's a wonderful photograph of the great dancer Bill (Bojangles) Robinson in Bojangles in the West End. There are other wall decorations ranging from photos to a fiddle in this busy spot with a neighbourhood feel. Comfortable seating inside and out with speciality coffees served hot or cold. There are sand-wiches and massive desserts ranging from cheesecakes to giant date squares. Bojangles is located at 785 Denman Street.

RIVER-DANCE CAFÉ: Sometimes coffee appears when you least expect it. Near the river at the foot of No. 2 Road, a husband and wife team operate a dance studio and coffee-house. There are the usual lattes and espressos and mochas along with appetizing banana-nut bread and triple-berry almond squares, sandwiches and soup. It's not just a morning place—on Saturday nights you can find some pretty decent jazz here as well. The River-Dance Café is located at 10-13040 No. 2 Road in Richmond.

GREAT WAYS TO
HANG ONTO SUMMER

BY GLEN SCHAEFER

It seems that once the kids are back in school and summer is offi-
cially "over," the great weather begins. As soon as the Labour Day
Weekend passes, the sun comes out for what seems like a permanent
vacation in Vancouver. As we hurry to our appointments, classes and
meetings, it mocks us with its beckoning rays. We're not recommend-
ing that anybody play hooky but, if you can wangle a break, we have
ten great ways to hang onto summer.

FLY A KITE: Gastown's Kites on Clouds toy store (131 Water
Street) says the return of kids to schools is a downdraft on
the summer kite trade. There's always a big selection of these

great aerial toys, from $7 single-line kites to $50 big box kites. To make the most of your kite-flying experience, there's a crisp breeze off English Bay toward West Vancouver's Ambleside Park most days. Vanier Park in Kits is a kiter's mecca, and the sands at White Rock's beach give a lot of room to stretch your wings.

BUY AN ICE-CREAM CONE: From the basic Dairy Queen soft cone to the exotic taste of champagne sorbet, there are plenty of ice-cream parlours in Vancouver to suit everyone's cravings. Try Mario's Gelati Italian Ice Cream at 88 East 1st Street for the ultimate Vancouver gelati experience.

GRIND IT: North Vancouver's mountainside thigh-burner of a hike, the Grouse Grind, has new hours to go with September's fading daylight. After reaching the top, take some time to look down and gaze at Vancouver in all of its sunny splendour.

RENT A CONVERTIBLE: Exotic Car Rentals at 1820 Burrard in Vancouver has a BMW, a Ferrari 355 Spyder and various Vipers and Porsches in between for daily rentals. Manager Larry Reid says the Whistler highway is usually the destination of choice and there's no telling who'll come in to rent a Ferrari. "We had a lady in a while ago, she must have been about 65 or 70. She just had to get it out of her system."

GO TO A DRIVE-IN MOVIE: Surrey's Hillcrest (18694 Fraser Highway) shows first run movies. Pile the kids in their car with their pyjamas on, bring their sleeping bags, and stare at the stars if the movie leaves you cold.

PLAY BASEBALL: Make use of all of the school fields lying unused in the still-light evenings. Grab a bunch of friends for a pick-up game and do your best imitation of the boys of summer. If you can't get enough people together, grab a friend and just play catch. There's nothing like baseball to define summer.

PEOPLE WATCH: Haul up a streetside cafe seat and check the pedestrian parade. Males and females in body-hugging summer gear have spent the past months swimming, boarding or Grouse-grinding and they've never looked better. Just weeks from now, they'll be buried under layers of scarves, sweaters and jackets until spring. So enjoy. Just wear your sunglasses and try to be discreet.

BARBECUE SOMETHING: Wear the funny apron. Swat at flies with your spatula. Douse the steak with a bit of that beer you're holding in your hand. Toss the football. Pass the potato salad. Eat charred meat. This is your last chance at singed eyebrows this year.

SUNTAN: Get onto the porch for a last tanning session with one of those foil reflectors under your chin. Yes, doctors frown on suntanning any time, but you can stay out longer at this time of year than at high summer. "As the sun's angle changes, there's more protection from UV rays but sunscreen is still a good idea, pretty well into the late fall," says dermatologist Dr. Joanna Day.

GO CANOEING: Get all Canadian in the definitive Great White North water transportation. Indian Arm's always nice and there are rentals at Deep Cove's Panorama Park. If kayaking's more your style, check out Granville Island Boat Rentals Ltd. (682-6287) for kayak rentals. Then slip into False Creek for a decidedly different view of Vancouver's downtown core.

GREAT PLACES TO GO ANTIQUING

By Mike Roberts

The Lower Mainland boasts hundreds and hundreds of antique stores and several antique malls and "rows" well known to professional and amateur collectors for their unique and unusual offerings. Here are a list of ten antique stores that are off the beaten track, yet come highly recommended by *Province* readers.

TONY'S: This is the one-stop antique shop for the home renovator or restoration buff. You need it, Tony's got it, from antique bathtubs and plumbing fixtures to classy vintage chandeliers and the largest collection of antique doorknobs in the world. The 25-year-old shop also carries wood carvings from around the world, including an impressive collection of Kenyan masks and First Nations works from the Pacific Northwest. Tony's is located at 3662 West 4th Avenue in Vancouver.

ANTIQUE EXCHANGE: Vancouverites agree that owners Wayne and Susan Corbett know their stuff when it comes to unique collectibles. And, they are quick to add, items are priced to sell. The shop is bright and spacious and the stock is well displayed for the curious browser. It carries a bit of everything, from collectible knick-knacks and old furniture to original war helmets and turn-of-the-century carpets. If you're on the lookout for antique glassware, this is a shop worth noting. The Antique Exchange is located at 20560 Langley Bypass in Langley.

FLEETWOOD ANTIQUES ETC.: Are you looking for a certain something to add pizzazz to a room in your house? Fleetwood Antiques will provide. Sisters Lynn Baxter and Louise Chamberlin took over the old Chinese restaurant in 1996 and took advantage of the rustic building's sectioned layout, using each section for a different theme of antiques or collectibles. The sisters sell old farm equipment, tools, gardening gear, hardware for the house, antique kitchen utensils, furniture, lanterns, tea caddies, etchings, mirrors and wonderful old gilt frames. Fleetwood Antiques Etc. is located at 15901 Fraser Highway in Surrey.

THE PEG GENERAL STORE LTD.: Owner Bruce Shaw has been on location coming on eight years and says he specializes in "eclectic accessories" like "weird lamps" and "unusual side tables." Vintage furniture is one of the store's mainstays and The Peg's collection of reasonably priced free-standing wardrobes are popular with local antiquers. Most items date from the 1930s to the present. Although Shaw says he stocks a lot of old English treasures and silver and china, most of his wares are vintage items from the 1950s, '60s and '70s. The Peg General Store Ltd. is located at 1003 Commercial Drive in Vancouver.

HIDDEN TREASURES: It's well worth the trip up the Sea-to-Sky Highway to browse through the treasures in David and Chrys Feth's quaint little store. The shop features hundreds of collectibles from the early 1950s, furniture, jewellery, ornaments and antique linens. The current owners took possession of the store in 1997 and began specializing in early 1950s collectibles. Even so, the store's collection of ladies hats dating from the 1920s to 1940s is impressive enough that movie industry costume scouts have been stopping by to buy. Hidden Treasures is located at 38036 Cleveland Avenue in Squamish.

SHIP TO SHORE NAUTICAL ANTIQUES: In the market for some maritime antiques? Drop anchor at Ship to Shore and take stock of the amazing collection of nautical antiques Ole Schmidt has amassed at his small shop near Lonsdale Quay. Brass lamps, chronometers, sextants and diving helmets are just some of the original antiques on Schmidt's shelves. He also carries ship models, bells and books and his favourite gem, the compass and steering wheel of the North Vancouver Ferry No. 4, which ran from 1931 to 1958 where the SeaBus sails today. Ship to Shore Nautical Antiques is located at 7A Lonsdale Avenue in North Vancouver.

HOMETOWN ANTIQUES: This antique store has something for everyone in the market for the old and special collectible. Verna Davies' shop is packed with antique bone china and unique glassware, but furniture is her favourite type of antique to collect and sell. "I have a lot of Canadian oak from the turn of the century," says Davies. Hometown Antiques is located at 5764-176th Street in Cloverdale.

FARMHOUSE COLLECTIONS: Owners Kelly King and Haward Palmateer specialise in Eastern Canadian antiques— turn-of-the-century furniture from Quebec and Ontario. Can't afford the original? The proprietors do a swift trade in pine reproductions, which they say are very popular with Vancouverites. Aside from furniture, Farmhouse Collections has a wide-ranging selection of antiques for the home and garden (including old tools, cast iron urns and planters). Farmhouse Collections is located at 2915 Granville Street in Vancouver.

NAPIER'S COUNTRY ANTIQUES: Owner Ken Napier got into the antiques game at the age of 19. That was over 30 years ago. Together with wife Nancy, Napier imports antiques direct from England, the U.S. and Indonesia, including a stellar collection of Victoria-era teak furniture. "As it's found, that's how I sell it," says Ken Napier. "I don't restore—unless the customer requests it." The Napiers' store is literally packed to the roof with the quaint, elegant and exotic. The shop stocks hardware and furniture throughout and boasts 300 to 400 stained glass windows, 200 to 300 mirrors dating from the 1850s to the Deco period and 50 to 60 vintage radios. Napier's Country Antiques is located at 6743-216th Street in Langley.

CASH'S NEW AND USED HOME FURNISHINGS: Fay and Dave Cash have been in business for over 25 years and carry an assortment of furnishings, accessories and unusual knick-knacks. The stock is always changing at the Cash's shop as customers snap up old pictures, lamps, ornaments and vintage bric-a-brac. The old dressers and antique beds got a special mention from *Province* readers, who said if you're in the refinishing game, Cash's is a place you might want to visit. Cash's New and Used Home Furnishings is located at 154 West 3rd Street in North Vancouver.

GREAT GROCERY STORES

By Glen Schaefer

The best way to enjoy a city and escape the usual over-priced tourist attractions is to enter a local grocery store. Not only will you save money on dining out, but you'll also get a unique glimpse at the "true" local fare of Vancouver.

Vancouver has an amazing variety of grocery stores—from the upscale to the chain-operated supermarket to the Mom and Pop corner stores. Here are ten of the best.

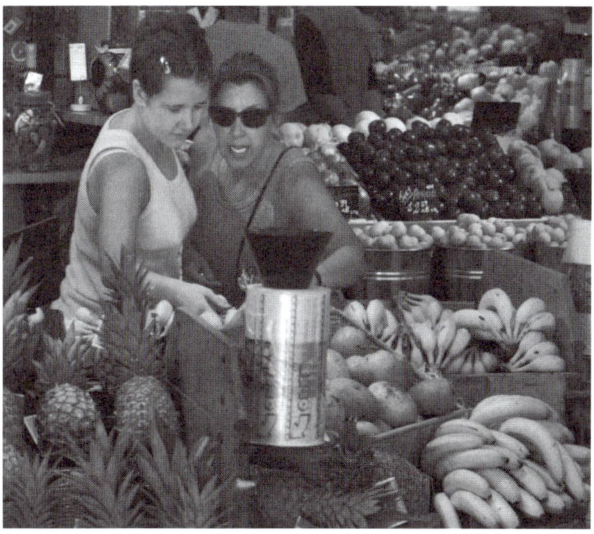

URBAN FARE: Situated just a gull's wing flap from False Creek among the new and under-construction high-end condos, Urban Fare represents a new high-end destination for grocery shopping in Vancouver. It offers a licensed lounge next to an array of bewildering gourmet stuff (what exactly is lemongrass ginger oil and what do you do with it?) and gorgeous vegetables laid out like jewellery-store pearls. If you have to look at the price tags, you can't afford it. Urban Fare is located at 177 Davie Street in Vancouver.

MEINHARDT FINE FOOD: This is the store that blazed the pricey trail now being followed by Urban Fare. It's a style that was, in turn, borrowed from stores in Manhattan's upper east side. On the "hipness" scale, Meinhardt is trendy enough to rate a mention in a short story by Zsu Zsi Gartner, a local author who has garnered national acclaim. Meinhardt Fine Food is located at 3002 Granville Street.

SUPERSTORE: As big stores go, this one's bigger than most, with a colour scheme of bright yellow splashed with green. Get a sense of the earth's curvature as you roll your buggy the 3 kilometres (approximately 1 mile) to the produce section. Brand selection thins out past President's Choice (the in-store brand) but it's hard not to take loopy joy in a store that expands the definition of groceries to include car batteries, luggage sets and rocking chairs. Superstore is located in Metrotown at 4800 Kingsway Avenue in Burnaby.

SAVE-ON-FOODS: Just a squeaky-wheel turn round the Metrotown corner from its chief competitor is this outlet of British Columbia mega-dealer Jimmy Pattison's grocery empire. Similar idea to Superstore except more colourful. There's a case-lot section in one corner where forklifts stack crates of fabric softener to the ceiling. A moving walkway takes shoppers up to a multi-level parking lot. Save-On-Foods is in Station Square at 6200 McKay Avenue in Burnaby.

OSAKA SUPER MARKET: Part of the Asian-flavoured T and T grocery chain, this is the supermarket to go to for live seafood, so your entrée can get a look at you while you get a look at it. Chinese sweets mingle with the Danishes in the bakery section and there's cook-and-serve dim sum in the deli. Cantonese rock songs waft from loudspeakers down the gleaming aisles. Osaka Super Market is located at Yaohan Centre (3700 No. 3 Road) in Richmond.

SAFEWAY: Some outlets of this venerable chain have followed the mega-size way of Save-On and Superstore but this outlet at the foot of Mount Seymour has kept to a human scale. A walk through the aisles isn't a major hike. The store

gets a steady business from mountain bikers and others looking to stock up on bottled water and energy bars before hitting the slopes. You'll see the mud-spattered bikers post-ride
in the open plaza next to the store. Safeway is located in
Parkgate Village at 3650 Mount Seymour Parkway in North
Vancouver.

BUDGET FOODS: Cardboard is the decor theme in this
warehouse-style store. But part of the draw is the fact that
after you've stuffed your car trunk with 8-kilogram bags of
dry cat food and olive oil by the flat, you're in Ladner—a
folksy little riverside town with a charming main street and a
couple of sidewalk cafes nearby. Budget Foods is located at
126-4857 Elliot Road in Ladner.

CAPERS: Aimed at natural food lovers in the swish part of
town, Capers offers one of the best selections of organic food
in Vancouver. Pick up peanut-based African soups or extra-
virgin olive oil produced by former Greenpeace chair David
McTaggart on a farm in Umbria. International pop star Bryan
Adams has been spotted at this Dundarave store feeding his
vegan spirit. Capers is located at 2496 Marine Drive in West
Vancouver.

TRUFOODS: An excellent source of East Indian foods and
spices, the proprietors of Trufoods grind their own ginger
powder, hot chili powder and fresh garam masala, a fragrant
blend of cardamom, cinnamon, cloves, coriander, cumin and
black pepper. Shopping here is truly a sensual experience.
Trufoods is located at 10119-136A Street in Surrey.

FOOD TOWN: For every supermarket grocery store in
Vancouver, there are at least three Mom and Pop corner
stores. Food Town is the epitome of the corner store experience in Vancouver. We highlighted this store because just
once in every life, you should have coffee at a place called
Mom's, buy a car from a guy named Honest Ed and get a jug
of milk at a place called Food Town. Food Town is located at
9583-132nd Street in Surrey.

GREAT PUMPKIN PATCHES

By Melissa Radler

Halloween is coming up and it seems that everywhere you look, black and orange decorate stores and homes with careless abandon. If you haven't got a pumpkin yet, don't despair. We've got ten great pumpkin patches for you to make your selection from. And if you're visiting the Lower Mainland around Halloween, don't be despondent over the lack of Halloween revelry that you can participate in. Go for a look at these amazing pumpkin fields, many of which offer hayrides and other fun attractions, and get back into the spirit of Halloween.

RICHMOND COUNTRY FARMS: With over 20 hectares (50 acres) of pumpkins, ranging up to over 45 kilograms (100 pounds) in weight, Richmond Country Farms is a pilgrimage site for many a pumpkin lover. Andrew Cawood, an early child educator at St. James Daycare, says "The pumpkins are sometimes bigger than the kids picking them." Tours include hayrides with singing cowboys and the Country Bumpkins live band. Richmond Country Farms is located at 12900 Steveston Highway in Richmond. Open Fridays 6:30 to 9 p.m. and weekends 10 a.m. to 4 p.m. Call 274-0522 for more information.

LAITY FARM: Laity Farm is over 125 years old and sports a huge variety of pumpkins for Halloween connoisseurs. "We have sugar pumpkins, the little ones for pies, kids on school tours pick medium ones and their dads come on the weekend—they want the big ones," says owner Heather Laity. Heather's son Doug who planted a tiny patch that netted $40 founded the pumpkin patch 15 years ago. Today, the pumpkin patch is over 3 hectares (8 acres) and much more profitable. Laity Farm is located at 21145-128th Avenue in Maple Ridge. Call 604-467-4302 for more information.

ALDOR ACRES: Aldor Acres has 6 hectares (15 acres) of pumpkins, with sizes ranging from the little pie pumpkins to 23-kilogram (50-pound) mammoths. Activities include hayrides to and from the patch and visits with the farm animals. Be sure to catch a glimpse of Aldor Acres' famous mascot, Big Bob, the gigantic 1,678-kilogram (3,700-pound) steer. Aldor Acres is located at 24990-84th Avenue in Langley. Call 604-888-0788 for more information.

WILLOW VIEW FARMS: Willow View Farms hosts an annual Pumpkin Daze, which features visits to the pumpkin patch and hayrides every 20 minutes. Kids will enjoy the playground and balloon typhoon while adults collect pumpkins up to 91 kilograms (200 pounds). The biggest pumpkin ever sold weighed in at a whopping 122 kilograms (269 pounds). Willow View Farms is located at 288 McCallum Road in Abbotsford. Call 604-854-8710 for more information.

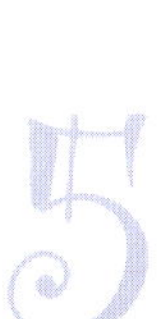

YELLOW BARN COUNTRY PRODUCE: The Great Pumpkin Hunt begins at the Yellow Barn. Hour-long hayrides atop a covered hay wagon are featured, with Farmer Alex and the Pumpkin Lady giving educational tours all the way to Pumpkin Land, a 2-hectare (5-acre) patch covered with pumpkins from grapefruit size to over 45 kilograms (100 pounds). The only rule here is that you have to carry your pumpkin out with you. Yellow Barn Country Produce is located at 39809 No. 3 Road in Abbotsford. Call 604-852-0888 for more information.

REYNELDA FARMS: This .2-hectare (half-acre) patch is open all the time, run by Janice and Stan Reynolds and their five sons Craig, Keith, Tyler, Derek and Mitchell. Filled with pumpkins up to 27 kilograms (60 pounds), locals and tourists stop by in droves to check out the patch and take pictures of the pumpkin and scarecrow display. Reynelda Farms is at 2485 Westham Island Road in Delta, near the bird sanctuary. Call 946-7152 for more information.

WESTHAM ISLAND HERB FARM: From babies to 36-kilogram (80-pound) monsters, pumpkins of all sizes are grown in this .2-hectare (half-acre) patch. The best time to visit this pumpkin patch is in the evening. In the spirit of Halloween, every year hundreds of pumpkins will be carved and lit up at night during the last week of October. Westham Island Herb Farm is located at 4690 Kirkland Road in Delta. Call 946-4393 for more information.

LEA LAKE FARMS: Lea Lake has 1.4 hectares (3.5 acres) of U-pick pumpkins, ranging from 22 grams to 27 kilograms (less than an ounce to 60 pounds), and a haywagon ride takes kids and adults straight to the field. "The pumpkins are great, but the real treat," says owner Wayne Oliver, "is that there's a hay maze and a corn maze for the kids to run through." Lea Lake Farms is located at 5100-72nd Street in Delta.

THOMCREST FARMS' APPLE AND PUMPKIN BARN: On this .8-hectare (2-acre) densely packed patch, pumpkins range from tiny babies to 40-kilogram (88-pound) wonders. Visitors can catch a hayride to the patch, offered every 15 minutes, or enjoy other activities such as a petting zoo, baby chicks, pony rides, goat skyway and scarecrow-making. The farm's 10,000 apple trees provide some spectacular sight-seeing. The biggest pumpkin ever sold here weighed in at

113 kilograms (249 pounds). Thomcrest Farms' Apple and Pumpkin Barn is located at 333 Gladwin Road in Abbotsford. Call 604-853-3108 for more information.

CHU LIN FARM: This pumpkin patch is open every day for the picking, with pumpkins ranging from 4 to 45 kilograms (9 to 100 pounds). The farm features chickens and ducks, which provide an amusing distraction during the serious business of choosing the perfect pumpkin. Children take what they can carry out…pumpkins, that is. Not chickens and ducks. Chu Lin Farm is located at 17535-40th Avenue in Surrey. Call 604-574-0268 for more information.

GREAT FALL PLEASURES

By Glen Schaefer

Short, grey days spent under overcoats and umbrellas, sunshine only in fits and starts, and little relief in sight…short of a plane ticket south. That's the dim view of fall in the Lower Mainland. But before resigning yourself to rainy purgatory, take the positive view: your risk of skin cancer goes way down, those minor figure flaws are smoothed over by turtleneck fashions and layers of rainwear, and the cool, damp air is as clean as it gets. There's just no end of silver linings in a place this cloudy.

WALK THROUGH THE AUTUMN LEAVES: Or if you're feeling energetic and have a rake handy, do some raking— the first time for that running leap into the middle of the pile and the second time for clean-up purposes. Depending on whether any children are about, the number of times raking up the same pile of leaves could be three, four, five…

CHECK OUT THE SEAWALL on a windy day and fell the power of air meeting water. There's nothing like a good frothy wave being bashed straight up and over the wall. Good sights include Stanley Park and West Vancouver between 14th Street and 24th Street.

IF YOU GO OUT IN THE WOODS TODAY you'll get a whiff of why this place is called the rainforest. Hit the trails and take a deep breath. That's the West Coast circle of life—the pungent reek of old trees, festooned with moss and mushrooms in a slow, damp decay to feed new trees. The University Endowment Lands/Pacific Spirit Park off 4th Avenue are an excellent spot for observing this natural cycle.

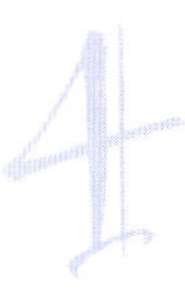

NOW THAT THERE ARE NO LIFEGUARDS TO YELL AT YOU, LET YOUR DOG RUN ON THE BEACH. Just don't leave anything behind for other beachcombers. Some good beaches to try: Dundurave Beach off Marine Drive in West Vancouver, or Jericho Beach off 4th Avenue in Vancouver.

THE FOG: It comes, it goes, sometimes in wispy swirls that circle you as you walk, sometimes in great thick blankets that you can see from up on a hill. For a great view, drive up to the Cypress Point lookout in West Vancouver to watch the city's bridges rise out of the fog like ships. Nothing beats getting a good look at the air before you breathe it. To get to the lookout, take Exit 8 off Highway 99.

GRAB A MUG OF SOMETHING HOT, plant yourself in a public place and do some people watching. Vancouver's three public markets (Granville Island, Lonsdale Quay, and Westminster Quay) are prime spots.

TURN YOUR FACE UP AND CATCH A BIT OF RAIN. All that moisture has to be good for your skin and a little trickle down the tongue never hurt. This is the freshest water you can find anywhere around.

 **WHY NOT TAKE A BRISK WALK?** A great meeting of hot and cold happens as you're appropriately bundled body warms up and the frigid air chills your face. Or find a partner and slow down a bit. It's always a surprise how a walk on a wet, grey day can be snug and warm if you're holding hands with someone.

 **ANYWHERE ELSE, WEARING HATS CAN BE A BIT OF FOPPY AFFECTATION,** but during a West Coast autumn, it's just practical. And we're not talking about shape-less toques to blunt an eastern-wind chill. No, for these parts you want the real deal: stylish, wide-brimmed felt suitable for a Bogart or a Bergman. Try Edie's Hats in the Net Loft Market at Granville Island. Here's looking at you, kid.

 **GET DIRTY!** Join mountain bikers in their mud-splattered clothing to gardeners up to their knees transplanting great huge rhododendrons to pre-schoolers stomping through their first mud puddles. The only thing that tops the satisfaction of a hard-layer of earth is a toasty soak in the tub to wash it off.

GREAT PLACES TO BUY PENNY CANDY

BY HARDIP JOHAL

Just the thought of an Everlasting Gob Stopper—among the fictional treats Charlie discovered in Willy Wonka's Chocolate Factory—is enough to make anyone's mouth water. But Roald Dahl's imagination isn't the only place to find irresistible sweets. Following are ten Great Stores—in no particular order—to visit in your quest for "penny" candy in the Lower Mainland.

CLAYBURN VILLAGE STORE: "The Great Wall of Candy award most definitely belongs to the Clayburn Village Store," says *Province* reader Wendy Harris. "They import penny candy from international destinations, especially Britain," says the Abbotsford resident. "A complete wall and two counters of the store are loaded up with jars of every type of candy imaginable!" For a dollar, you can fill up a brown paper bag worth of treats, just like in the good old days. The store is beautiful and worth a country drive for the nostalgia factor alone. The Clayburn Village Store is located at 34810 Clayburn Street in Abbotsford.

PORTER'S GENERAL STORE: Sometimes when you think about penny candy, it's the memory of the candy you enjoyed in your youth that tantalises your taste buds. Then a quick trip to the corner store reveals nothing like what you imagined satisfying your craving with. Porter's General Store is the antidote to those frustrated moments. They do a wonderful job tracking down those great goodies from the olden days for their old-fashioned candy counter. Porter's General Store is located at 21611-48th Avenue in Langley.

CIOFFI'S MEAT MARKET AND DELI: You can find an impressive selection of treats from overseas at Cioffi's Meat Market and Deli. An array of colourful jars contain Confetti, irresistible candy-coated almonds or chocolate that come in a rainbow of colours—plus silver and gold. Most popular with kids are the Fruitine, little fruit-flavoured hard candies. For more mature taste buds, there are chamomile, rhubarb and espresso-flavoured sweets. Other must-tries are Bajadera (a chocolate-covered truffle-like confection), almond nougat, the tiny but flavour-packed Limencino (lemon hard candy) and Ribes Nero (grape hard candy). Cioffi's Meat Market and Deli is located at 4156 Hastings Street in Burnaby.

THE CHOCOLATE MARKET: The Chocolate Market has made a strong impression on the sweet of tooth in the Lower Mainland. Located on the upper retail level of the Royal Centre Mall in downtown Vancouver (1055 West Georgia), The Chocolate Market offers 24 flavours of Jelly Bellys, including no-sugar-added Bellys and sour Bellys. Also available is an array of Gummy confections, including chocolate-covered Gummy Bears and white-chocolate-covered Polar Bears. Lovers of elusive Floral Gums will be thrilled to learn you can find them here. The Chocolate Market is located in Royal Centre Mall at 1055 West Georgia.

BEN'S MARKET: A nostalgic favourite in Vancouver and the Lower Mainland is Ben's Market. For kids in North Delta, Ben's was the place to stock up on liquorice whips, Fun Dip, Double Bubble and other treats. These days, the big sellers are Baby Bottle Pops (filled with sherbet), marshmallow bananas, and Sour Keys. Ben's Market is located at 9595-116th Street in North Delta.

7-ELEVEN: *Province* reader Barbara Valverde highly recommends 7-Eleven's expanded candy selection. "My favourite is the gummy teeth," says the New Westminster resident, who frequents the 7-Eleven on 12th Street in her city. Gummy teeth? "They're little teeth with gums made from Gummy Bear material," explains Valverde. She also favours little gummy fruits. 7-Eleven stores can be found throughout the Lower Mainland.

AVRIL'S SUGARLESS CANDY COMPANY: Tucked away on the upper level of Surrey Place Mall is a paradise for candy-lovers looking for sweets without the sugar. Surrey resident Sally Ann Ratcliffe, who has diabetes, makes frequent trips to Avril's Sugarless Candy Company for red liquorice and toffee, which can be bought by the piece or by the pound. For those looking to curb their sweet tooth without guilt, this is the place to be. Avril's Sugarless Candy Company is located in Surrey Place Mall on the corner of 102nd Avenue and King George Highway.

MAC'S: This is another chain of corner stores that easily satisfies the sweet tooth with penny candy. Most popular with kids are Coke Bottles, Fuzzy Peaches and Sour Keys, all for a nickel apiece. For adults, Mac's is open 24 hours to cater to that 3:00 a.m. sweet attack. Mac's stores can be found throughout the Lower Mainland.

SMILE & SHINE MARKET: This is a popular Coquitlam location that boasts a great selection of penny candy. For about a dollar, you can get three jumbo Gummy Frogs, 20 little strawberry marshmallows and a package of bubble gum. The Smile & Shine Market is located at 658 Clark Street in Coquitlam.

CANDY KITCHEN: At the Candy Kitchen in Granville Island Public Market you'll find a veritable Gummy zoo: Gummy Dolphins, Gummy Bulldogs and chocolate-covered Gummy Bears. You'll also find candy sticks in too many flavours to list here. The Candy Kitchen is located in the Granville Island Public Market underneath the Granville Street Bridge.

GREAT PLACES TO CLEAR YOUR MIND

By Glen Schaefer

They say looking at something—anything—green is a sure-fire way to clear the mind. That's why hospital gowns and operating rooms are usually green. That's also why people pour into parks after dinner for a calming walk but they couldn't tell you why. Views from great heights are a good mind-clearer as well. Despite the fact that Vancouver's got a plethora of green spots to head to, we thought we'd make it easier for you to decide where to go for some inner calm. Here are ten great Lower Mainland spots to clear the mind.

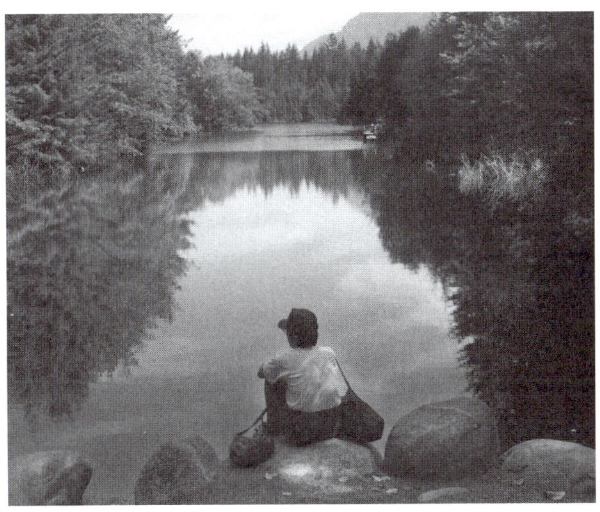

DR. SUN YAT-SEN CLASSICAL CHINESE GARDEN: A thousand years of understanding balance, symmetry and harmony have gone into this rendering of a Ming dynasty garden, built in 1985, with thick, high walls, carved camphor wood rafters, pools, streams and Asian plants. Try sitting or standing in one spot for as long as possible to allow the mind to relax. Every stone, plant, sightline and sound is

AUTUMN

designed to delight and soothe. The Dr. Sun Yat-Sen Classical Chinese Garden is located at 578 Carrall Street and open from 9:30 a.m. to 7 p.m. daily, including holidays.

GILBERT BEACH: *Province* reader Laura Chapotelle has been coming here for over 15 years every time she needs a quiet moment. "Old boat houses are moored, fish boats go along the south arm of the Fraser and you can see where they take the ferries to dry-dock. Somewhere underneath is the Massey Tunnel and it seems you could throw a rock and hit Ladner on the other side." Gilbert Beach is on Finn Slough Road, east of Steveston in Richmond.

THE RIVER ROAD DIKE: Looking across the Fraser River from here, you can watch the planes take off and land in the distance at Vancouver International Airport, with the North Shore mountains as a backdrop. The regular upward parade of big jets appears as a distant, delicate defiance of the law of gravity. Turn your gaze westward at sunset for the nightly show of colours over the gulf. The River Road Dike is located on the north-western tip of Richmond's Lulu Island.

WHITE ROCK ON THE END OF THE PIER: A whiff of the shallow sea mixes with the waft of fried foods from the shops on Marine Drive behind you. Looking out onto the expanse of Boundary Bay with the crowds behind you gives you a feeling of balance. If you stare hard enough at the sun on the water, the sounds of everyone else on the pier melts away, leaving you in your own oasis of calm. To get to White Rock, follow Highway 99.

DEER LAKE: Go around to the west side of the lake, where the Oakalla parksite rises behind you. Somewhere to the north is the rush of cars on Canada Way but not near enough to notice. This patch of calm in the middle of the city is so peaceful, it's hard to imagine it was the site of a prison. Deer Lake Park is located in Burnaby. Take the Deer Lake Parkway exit off Canada Way.

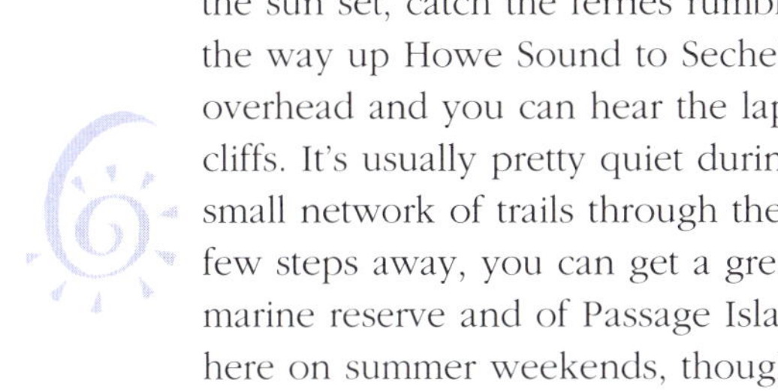**WHYTECLIFF PARK:** From a little viewing area you watch the sun set, catch the ferries rumbling by and look north all the way up Howe Sound to Sechelt. Eagles sometimes fly overhead and you can hear the lapping of waves on the cliffs. It's usually pretty quiet during the week. There is also a small network of trails through the gnarled pines and cliffs. A few steps away, you can get a great view of the ecological marine reserve and of Passage Island and Point Grey. No rest here on summer weekends, though, when it's extremely crowded. Whytecliff Park is located at Odlum Crescent and Rockland Wynd near Horseshoe Bay.

THE GRANVILLE STREET BRIDGE: Sometimes there's calm amidst the urban storm. Start out walking from either end of the bridge, get yourself to the midpoint, pause and take a look. Cars and buses go by but their speed separates them from you. A wind blows above False Creek and, far below, the grey bustle of the concrete plant churns alongside the multi-coloured jostling of market, restaurants and art school. The walk across the bridge, with a pause in the middle, can take a good 20 minutes.

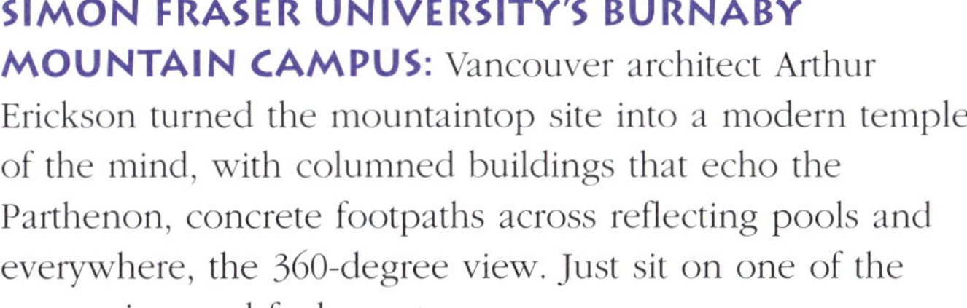**SIMON FRASER UNIVERSITY'S BURNABY MOUNTAIN CAMPUS:** Vancouver architect Arthur Erickson turned the mountaintop site into a modern temple of the mind, with columned buildings that echo the Parthenon, concrete footpaths across reflecting pools and everywhere, the 360-degree view. Just sit on one of the grassy rises and feel smarter.

**INDIAN ARM OFF DEEP COVE IN NORTH VANCOUVER:** For the ultimate in calm, get yourself a kayak. (You can rent one at Panorama Park.) Head north for a few kilometres and the roads are all gone. Stop paddling and just coast. At sunrise, you can watch the mountains light up while the sea birds' wing-beats are the only noise, along with the splash of the occasional harbour seal.

A HOUSE OF WORSHIP: Your church, temple or synagogue is there even when the weekly service isn't on. Whether it's Christ Church Cathedral, in the shadows of the downtown towers on Georgia Street, or a country chapel, there's a mind-clearing sanctuary to be had. For a sense of comforting nostalgia, try the two heritage churches on the corner of Nelson and Burrard.

GREAT PARKS

By Hardip Johal

Vancouver has no shortage of green space. Some parks enjoy international reputations and are crowded every weekend, no matter what the season. Others are tiny jewels that are hidden away and closely guarded by regular users. Whether it's quiet contemplation you seek or an afternoon of people-watching and hotdog-munching, there's a perfect spot somewhere out there for you to park yourself. Here are a list of ten great parks in Vancouver and the Lower Mainland.

PEACE ARCH PROVINCIAL PARK: "Look, Mommy, I'm in the U.S!" cries a little girl as she takes a flying leap on the manicured lawn of Peace-Arch Park. "Now I'm coming back to Canada!" The novelty of being able to jump—literally—from one country to the other has her giggling with delight. Created in the 1930s with money raised by Canadian and American school children, Peace Arch features playing fields, gardens, picnic shelters and playgrounds on both sides of the Surrey–Blaine border. To get to Peace Arch Provincial Park, head south on Highway 99.

REIFEL ISLAND BIRD SANCTUARY: This park is a bird-lover's paradise. Whether you're seeking to spot a rare species or just want to commune with nature, picturesque Reifel Island Migratory Bird Sanctuary fits the bill. Pathways stretch for 7 kilometres (approximately 4 miles) through the park. This is a popular spot for photographers, so be wary of walking into the viewfinder of a camera. Warming huts, blinds, lookouts and an observation tower allow you to observe nature at its finest without disturbing the natural habitat of the birds. To get to Reifel Island Bird Sanctuary, follow Ladner Trunk Road and watch for the sign pointing to Westham Island.

BELCARRA REGIONAL PARK: Beckoned by 9 kilometres (approximately 6 miles) of shoreline and views across Burrard Inlet to Deep Cove, park-goers fill the parking lots and picnic shelters of Belcarra on sunny weekends. But there's another side to this Port Moody park's personality that's best appreciated on a cool evening. With tranquil green spaces on one side and the waters of Indian Arm on the other, you can ramble along one of several wooded trails. Jug Island Trail provides a one-hour walk to Jug Island beach. At the end of the trail, you'll be rewarded by a vista of the mountains of Garibaldi Provincial Park. To get to Belcarra Regional Park, look for the sign on Ioco Road directing you to 1st Avenue.

ROCKY POINT PARK: *Province* reader Shannon Gombar has high praise for Rocky Point Park in Port Moody. "It's the best park going," says Gombar, a Port Moody resident who takes her dogs for daily walks in Rocky Point. "It starts with a playground, a wading pool and a big pool. There's a fish-and-chips place, a boat launch, a pier and trails that wind around the waterfront to another playground on the other side. There are also soccer fields and a fish hatchery." In addition to all of the above, Rocky Point is home to a stretch of the 16,000-kilometre Trans Canada Trail, which extends from Victoria, British Columbia, to St. John's, Newfoundland. Rocky Point Park is located off Murray Street in Port Moody.

MUNDY PARK: One of the largest tracts of urban park wilderness in BC, Mundy Park includes two lakes and a forest of Douglas Firs whose average age is 105 years. The park's 1.8 square kilometres (450 acres)—79% of which are forested—contain a playground, a soccer field and a baseball diamond as well as towering trees. On the walking and biking trails that wind through the forest, you can banish city sights—and most of the sounds—without actually leaving the city of Coquitlam. Mundy Park is located at the corner of Foster and Hillcrest streets in Coquitlam.

DEAS ISLAND REGIONAL PARK: Nestled in the south arm of the Fraser River in Delta, Deas Island boasts several unique features: the island is home to a restored heritage schoolhouse and Burrvilla, a heritage house. (They're open on special occasions.) And there's plenty of sandy beach for exploration and castle construction. Deas Island Regional Park is located off River Road in Delta.

WHYTECLIFF PARK: As you pull up in the parking lot you'll see a pleasant but unremarkable lawn and play-ground—but that's the least of what makes this West Vancouver park a great getaway. From the cliff that leads down to the beach there are stunning views across Howe Sound at the Strait of Georgia. Rock stairways ease the walk down to the beach. Accessible at low tide—for adventurous types only—is Whyte Island, separated from the main shoreline by a rocky bar. Check the morning newspaper for tide tables. Whytecliff Park is located at Odlum Crescent and Rockland Wynd near Horseshoe Bay.

QUEEN'S PARK: Ken McEwen, a New Westminster *Province* reader, cites the children's playground—complete with water park and petting zoo—the formal gardens, tennis courts, basketball courts and baseball diamonds as evidence that this is a "perfect park." "There are lovely picnic areas, shady walks and lawns to lollygag on," says McEwen. "Queen's Park is truly a community focal point and gathering spot. It's also a neat place to walk the dog." To access Queen's Park, enter off McBride Boulevard or at 1st Street and 3rd Avenue in Vancouver.

 **STANLEY PARK:** This icon of Vancouver has produced some memorable images over the years: a bikini-clad—and diapered—toddler ventures hesitantly into the cold spray of the water park before falling in love with the splashes all around her; a little boy jumps up and down with anticipation before boarding the miniature train; content grandparents push strollers along the seawall. Stanley Park is truly a park for all generations. The best time to enjoy it without having to contend with crowds is early in the morning. Stanley Park is located at the west end of downtown Vancouver. Enter on Beach Avenue or off Georgia Street.

 **BARNETT MARINE PARK:** *Province* reader Danny George describes Burnaby's Barnett Marine Park as "a mini French Riviera." The park's peaceful atmosphere and the view of sailboats making their way along Burrard Inlet inspire George's admiration. This park is particularly beautiful in the evening and makes an excellent after-dinner destination. Barnett Marine Park is located off the Barnett Highway in Burnaby.

GREAT TOBOGGAN AND TUBING HILLS

By Glen Schaefer

TOBOGGAN. *n*. A long light narrow sledge, for sliding downhill esp. over compacted snow and ice. (Canadian French *tabaganne* from Algonquian)—*Concise Oxford Dictionary*

A bit of linguistic history for you. They don't tell us the Algonquian for "Ohmygawd, we're airborne," a phrase that would have helped for a few seconds on a recent fog-shrouded day of tubing at Mount Seymour. Fortunately "oooff" takes a pretty literal translation in any language. The lengths we go to research ten great toboggan and tubing hills for you. Some helpful hints: shoes or boots with a grip are a good idea. Nothing like trying to slither your way back uphill in last year's worn runners. Also, respect private property. If there's a fence, don't jump it.

MOUNT SEYMOUR: A supervised snow-play area allows sliders and toboggans, but no sleds with steering. Krazy Carpets and toboggans can be rented for the day if you don't have your own. A recent addition to this hill is a separate snow-tube park with a rope tow to save tubers the walk uphill. Try it on a day when there's a light fog, and treat your kidneys to a pounding on the invisible bumps near the bottom of the hill. The tube hill is wide enough to allow several tubers to go down alongside one another. Also, the hill is lit up for night tubing on weekends. For information on hours and rates, call 986-2261.

CYPRESS MOUNTAIN: They offer tobogganing at Cypress on Canada Day if there's enough snow, although that's a once-in-a-blue-moon thing. Still, you can count on sliding there until April anyway. Cypress has three courses side by side—one for tubers and two for toboggans, as well as a free smaller slope for smaller children. Recently, the hill was fitted with a new tubing lift that's off-limits to tobogganers. For information on hours and rates, call 926-5612.

HEMLOCK VALLEY: There are no toboggans allowed on this Fraser Valley ski area, but they will rent you a tube for a day. There's no tube-tow here, so ascents are made the organic way, lugging your own tube and those of your smaller co-tubers. No lights either, so tubing wraps up about 4:30 p.m. For information on hours and rates, call 604-797-4411.

QUEEN ELIZABETH PARK: On really cold days, Vancouver folks can toboggan closer to home for free. When snow blankets the city's higher reaches, Queen Elizabeth Park is a slider's paradise, bringing back memories of unregulated days on small-town hills. Queen Elizabeth Park is between Cambie and Main Street in Vancouver.

JERICHO HILL: On those still rarer days when the chill reaches to the lower Point Grey area of Vancouver, Jericho Hill turns into a tobogganers' paradise. This hill is regulated by the honour system, so take your turn.

THE DIKES ALONG THE RIVER IN MAPLE RIDGE: This free tobogganing and tubing site offers even-sloped, low-impact tobogganing for the younger thrill-seeker. Just be sure to slide down the landward side of the dike. There's nothing worse than being cold and wet. To reach the dikes along the river in Maple Ridge, follow the Lougheed Highway out of Vancouver.

ABBOTSFORD: Further out the valley, there's a nice rolling stretch of hills that's walking distance behind Abbotsford's Sandy Hill Elementary School. Apart from being free, the added bonus to this location is that the hills here roll enough for some good air time on the right sled. Sandy Hill Elementary School is located at 3836 Old Clayburn Road in Abbotsford.

MANNING PARK: What a deal—get a toboggan hill that's as big as the ones at Seymour or Cypress, but without the crowds. And it's free. The hill at the lower parking lot of the Gibson's Pass Ski area, about 10 kilometres (approximately 6 miles) from Manning Park's lodge on Highway 3, is wide enough for five toboggans to go down at the same time. It's unsupervised but it's getting more popular all the time, and more tobogganers could someday mean rules and a ticket booth. Call 250-840-8836 for information about conditions.

BIG BAR GUEST RANCH: A lot of Cariboo guest ranches stay open in the winter. Big Bar has trails for cross-country skiing and snowshoeing, a separate area for snowmobiling as well as horseback riding and sleigh rides. There's dog-sledding, skating and—yes—tobogganing. Take Highway 1, then 97 or Highway 99 via Whistler and Lillooet to Clinton. The BC Guest Ranchers Association is at 250-374-6836 or www.guestranches.com. The Cariboo-Chilcotin-Coast Tourism Association is at 1-800-663-5885.

PLAYDIUM: If you just don't like cold, wet feet, stay indoors. Playdium, the virtual-gamers' hangout at Burnaby's Metrotown Centre, has a game called Power Sled. It's a virtual toboggan ride that has the sled tilt 45 degrees as it goes through corners. It's speedy, warm and dry. Metrotown Centre is located at 4800 Kingsway in Burnaby.

GREAT WINTER DAY TRIPS

By David Spaner

Vancouver is great, but some days you just have to get away from things. Unfortunately, there are minor details like time off of work and budgets to deal with. The ideal solution is the day trip. These are the perfect solution to the mid-winter blahs, and the best part about these trips is you get to return to your own bed at the end of the day.

FORT LANGLEY: Not to be confused with the township and the city, this is small-town Canadiana at its best. The main drag's old wooden storefronts house galleries and antique shops alongside urbane coffee places. This was the spot where BC was declared a colony in 1858. The fort itself was a trading post, dismantled in the 19th century. It was rebuilt for BC's centennial in 1958, a time when Westerns were all the rage. Its high wooden walls enclose a blacksmith shop, big house and other buildings circa Canada's not-so-wild west. To reach Fort Langley, take Highway 1 eastward out of Vancouver and watch for the signs directing you to Fort Langley.

STEVESTON: Drive to southern Richmond and you're in Steveston, once a Japanese-Canadian community that housed the largest commercial fishing fleet in the world. It's still Canada's biggest fishing port and you can purchase fresh seafood off the boats on weekends. It also offers a riverfront walkway, and the galleries, restaurants and museums of Moncton Street, which often plays Main Street, U.S.A., in movies shot here.

GIBSONS: A short jaunt from Horseshoe Bay and you're standing on the site of 19 years of *The Beachcombers'* episodes. Check out Molly's Reach, the focus of that venerable CBC series. For those of you who could never stand *The Beachcombers,* the town offers other attractions, including marina, beach, restaurants, fish market and pioneer museum.

HARRISON HOT SPRINGS: Two springs from nearby mountains provide visitors with plenty of 38° Celsius (100° Fahrenheit) pools. The main attraction is the Harrison Hot Springs Hotel, which has pools, massages, a restaurant, and garden grounds to explore. If the Harrison Hot Springs Hotel isn't in your budget, the town has public hotsprings for your enjoyment.

WHITE ROCK: Fish, chips and a huge white rock. It all makes for a nice outing, especially when you consider that White Rock also has a great beach drive and eclectic shops. If you get tired of all things commercial, Crescent Beach provides a nice antidote to shopping and sightseeing.

VICTORIA: Funny thing about Victoria, a lot of tourists think it's a slice of England, but get away from a small section of downtown and it's pretty much like any Canadian city. If you want to play along, however, enjoy some afternoon tea at the Empress Hotel, take in the wax museum and go for a wild ride in a carriage. Leave early enough and you'll have time to stop at the world-famous Butchart Gardens on the way into town. Victoria is located on southern Vancouver Island. Ferries depart from Tsawwassan daily.

STANLEY PARK: If you don't live in Vancouver or even if you do, Lord Stanley's park is never a bad day trip. You've got wild squirrels and birds, an aquarium and a lagoon, Prospect Point and Brockton Point, a lumberman's log and a hollow tree. There are plenty of ways to tour the park: drive, inline skate, bike, jog or go by miniature train. The park boasts good restaurants and beaches, too. Stanley Park is located in the west end of downtown Vancouver. Enter off Georgia Street.

ANMORE-BELCARRA-IOCO: Visiting this area just past Port Moody is the closest thing to going to a Gulf Island without having to endure a ferry wait. There are beaches, horseback riding and plenty of country roads. While Anmore and Belcarra capture the island look, Ioco has a bit of that *X-Files* ambience. Driving toward town along Ioco Road, the first indication that you may have entered the *Twilight Zone* is a sign, "Pleasantside Grocery," on an aged general store with not much in it, except videos and chips. Arrive in the old oil company town and the only way you know you're in the 21st century, or even the 20th, is by looking at licence plates. The sparse houses (some boarded up) and everything else in Ioco looks like it's straight out of 1905.

BELLINGHAM: Bellingham is America to many in the Lower Mainland—the first taste they had of the U.S. It's quite a town. Bellingham has shopping and blue mailboxes and, well, shopping. There are detours along the way (Blaine), attractions to its south (La Conner) and a great, twisting, cliff-hanging Sunday drive (Chuckanut Drive). Mostly, though, Bellingham has always been about shopping. For years, it was the downtown and Bon Marche, then the Bellis Fair Mall. You wonder, though, if this Vancouver tradition has lost a little lustre now that the spirit of Bellingham seems to live in every Canadian mall too. Bellis Fair Mall is located at Bellis Fair Parkway in Bellingham, 40 kilometres (25 miles) south of the Canadian–American border.

NEW YORK: Enough with the rustic stuff, already. Now, let's just imagine a 24-hour trip to New York. Canadian Airlines departs Vancouver at 10:50 p.m., arrives in Toronto at 6:10 a.m., and a flight reaches New York at 8:35 a.m. Grab a cab into Manhattan and you've got time for the first act of a play, half a slice of pizza, a bite of a knish, a sip of chocolate egg cream, a ride halfway up the Empire State building, a look at the Statue of Liberty, postcards at the Modern Museum of Art, a walk around a Greenwich Village block, a one-stop ride on a subway and maybe a mugging. Flight leaves New York at 5 p.m. Back in Vancouver at 10:02 p.m.

GREAT PLACES TO GET HOT CHOCOLATE

By Lorne Mallin

Hot chocolate is one of those comfort foods that evoke memories of congregating in the kitchen after playing the snow. After we warmed our hands on the steaming mugs, the hot, sweet, milky flavour sliding down the throat made us feel so nourished inside. There's nothing like it to take the edge off winter weather.

HOLLYBURN LODGE: The hot chocolate here is hot with cross-country skiers and snowshoers on Cypress Mountain. For the ultimate hot chocolate experience, take the two-hour Hollyburn Meadows Tour which wends its way over forested snowshoe trails to the rustic lodge where guides will serve you with large cups of hot chocolate as you gaze up at the starlit sky. Call 922-0825 for information on Hollyburn Lodge.

BEAN AROUND THE WORLD: This homey coffeehouse, in West Vancouver's Ambleside, serves up a massive 20-ounce bowl of hot chocolate. It begins with a generous shot of chocolate syrup, followed by steamed milk and a dollop of foam, all topped with swirls of chocolate syrup and sprinkles of cocoa powder. Bean Around the World is located at 1522 Marine Drive in West Vancouver. Other locations in downtown Vancouver: 4456 West 10th Avenue and 2977 Granville Street.

DELANY'S IN THE VILLAGE: This is a popular spot in Edgemont Village in North Vancouver. The hot chocolate may not be as rich as some other places, but the setting is comfy, especially the stools with big wooden swivel seats. What's special here is the healthy serving of whipping cream and the 95-cent cup for children ten and under. Delany's in the Village is located at 3089 Edgemont Boulevard. If you're in the West End, check out Delany's at 1105 Denman Street.

GHIRADELLI SODA FOUNTAIN AND CHOCOLATE SHOP: This is Vancouver's outpost of a time-honoured chocolate institution in San Francisco. It feels like a soda fountain from another era, compete with classic rock on the sound system and a uniformed soda jerk behind the counter. Mini-marshmallows melt into the cocoa for a decidedly campfire-style flavour. You can also buy their sweet chocolate and powder to attempt to recreate the flavour at home. Ghiradelli Soda Fountain and Chocolate Shop is located at 1132 Robson Street.

DE DUTCH PANNEKOEK HOUSE: There are 13 branches of this breakfast-restaurant chain located throughout the Lower Mainland, all with a friendly, home-style atmosphere and massive platters of food. Served in De Mug, their hot chocolate was the hottest one we tried. Some downtown De Dutch Pannekoek House locations worth checking out are 1-1725 Robson Street and 2622 Granville Street. Check a local phone book for other locations throughout Vancouver and the Lower Mainland.

TORREFAZIONE COLIERA: This little gem on Commercial Drive has built its reputation on superb coffee, but they also serve a pretty mean hot chocolate. The atmosphere is very homey and unhurried. The hot chocolate is made with chocolate syrup, steamed milk and chocolate whipped cream. Torrefazione is located at 2206 Commercial Drive.

THE WELL ON DUNBAR: This West Side neighbourhood coffee and smoothie bar is the home of what is considered by many Vancouverites as the best hot chocolate in the city. Chocolate syrup and steamed milk are followed by chocolate mint whipped cream drizzled with chocolate and caramel syrup. The piece de resistance is a small log of solid chocolate that sits on top of the cup. The result is rich and chocolately. The Well on Dunbar is located at 3271 Dunbar Street.

DEATH BY CHOCOLATE: Immerse yourself in a total chocolate experience at this attractive chain of dessert-restaurants. It's easy to be overwhelmed by their amazing desserts, but the hot chocolate is worth a visit as well. There's plenty of variation on the hot-chocolate theme, including Double Chocolate and Chocolate Hazelnut. Death By Chocolate is located at 818 Burrard Street and 1001 Denman Street downtown, and other locations throughout the city. Check a local telephone book for addresses.

THE GRIND & GALLERY COFFEE BAR: This 24-hour East Side place has an antiquey, artsy feel. The smooth chocolate flavour is a little subtle—more like steamed milk with a touch of chocolate. The art on the walls is a visual feast. Located in the middle of Antique Row, this is the perfect spot to relax between antique stores. The Grind is located at 4124 Main Street.

THE PUB AT BRIDGES: For something different, try hot chocolate in a pub. This location, in the heart of Granville Island, provides an oasis from the sometimes-hectic market area. The hot chocolate is made from a mix and canned whipped cream, but the view and the relaxed atmosphere (leather couches and a fireplace) make this a popular destination. The Pub at Bridges is located at 1696 Duranleau on Granville Island.

GREAT THINGS TO DO WITH THE KIDS OVER THE CHRISTMAS HOLIDAY

By Glen Schaefer

Sure, you've been hearing that it's beginning to look a lot like Christmas since well before the kids finished off the Halloween candy, but now the season is well and truly upon us. Yuletide kicks into gear when schools let out, so the appropriate spirit is required. No more grousing about how the season is ruled by greed and commercialism, no more whining about mall crowds. It's time to get into the kid-friendly Christmas spirit, get a bit of that childlike wonder back into you. Try some of our ten great things to do with the children over the holidays. If you don't have any of your own—kids, that is— borrow some from a friend or a relative. It will probably be the best Christmas gift you can give them!

GO CAROLLING: Get some kids and grown-ups together and do the neighbourhood circuit. Run through a few carols before heading out, just to get them right. The adventurous can try harmonies. The mood is enhanced by the full carolling fashions—warm clothes, toques, scarves, and maybe a few candles held by the tallest of folks. And if a few people invite you in for shortbread and eggnog along the way, so much better.

BELIEVE IN SANTA: If that's hard to do, don't blow things for the believers when you pass by a half-a-dozen guys in Santa suits on any given outing. Here's the story: Santa is very busy this time of year, so he needs a lot of helpers who look just like him.

BEDTIME STORIES: *'Twas the Night Before Christmas* for the pre-schoolers, *A Child's Christmas in Wales* for the older ones. Put a little music in your voice, paint a picture with the words. Maybe distract a squirmy kid with a mandarin orange to give yourself a little time for the words to work their magic.

DO SOMETHING FOR OTHERS: In the few days before Christmas, get together with friends and family and do something for others. Call the United Way or the Christmas Bureau about agencies that could use a hand delivering packages or with other tasks. Or maybe there's a house-bound person living in your neighbourhood who could use a plate of cookies. Get the kids—and yourselves—thinking of others.

SLEEP: Sleep in on the morning of December 25th. Just kidding.

JOIN THE PLAY: Don't just watch—participate. Sit down on the floor with the kids and help make the puzzle, or get your Monopoly strategy back, take Barbie for a spin in her 'Vette, or play with the latest stuffed animal. Heading outdoors, don't be shy about trying out the new toboggan. But, as you tell the kids all the time, remember to share.

GO SKATING: Lower Mainlanders will have to do with the rinks at recreation facilities, and unstable folks who haven't strapped on blades for a while should watch out for those pint-sized demons doing their best imitations of NHL players.

In colder climes, the full outdoor scarf-and-campfire experience is a possibility, depending on the weather and the ice thickness. This is not something to be unsure about—check with local authorities before hitting the pond.

AFTERNOON MOVIES: A kid-sized bag of popcorn, dim the lights, and get yourself two hours of peace amid the seasonal bustle. The Christmas season is always highlighted by fantastic children's movies. Suspend your belief and enjoy. As a bonus, take advantage of the cheaper matinee rates (until 5:00 p.m) over the school holidays. To make the most of your movie experience, try the Metropolis theatre at Metrotown Centre, located at 4800 Kingsway in Burnaby.

THANK-YOU CARDS: To Granny for the new computer game, Aunt Mabel for the hand-knitted sweater. Maybe get the children some personal stationary in currently popular motif as an incentive. As to those thank-yous, you know the drill: in their own handwriting, more than one sentence, some personal detail and colour.

NEW YEAR'S EVE: Ever consider a change from the overblown cheer of a grown-ups' party? Greet the New Year with the kids. Play Twister in the early evening. Rent *The Party* with Peter Sellers. Eat popcorn and toast the New Year with a glass of sparkling pop. Watch the eyelids droop as you countdown the minutes and guess who'll be asleep at the stroke of midnight, you or them.

GREAT SHOPPING MALLS

By Melissa Radler

A day at the mall is a concept that has seeped into our culture over the years, and Vancouver shoppers certainly have quite a large selection of malls to choose from. Today's shopper need not venture far and wide to choose from hundreds of stores, consume endless soft drinks and fries and clothe him- or herself for eternity, all under one roof. Whether it's a great food court, stunning architecture or just the usual stores and boutiques, somewhere out there, there is a mall for you.

PARK ROYAL: The signs say "Shop By the Sea" and the air inside is 100% natural. It's actually a pleasure to spend the entire day inside this shopping metropolis perched just beneath West Vancouver's rolling hills—no headaches or watery eyes and double the fun with stores on both sides of the street. Park Royal Shopping Mall is located on the 700 Block of Marine Drive in West Vancouver.

METROTOWN: With more than 220 stores, movie theatres and a SkyTrain connection, Metrotown is the classic suburban hangout. You can spend a day in here and keep the family happily occupied. Parents can check out the boutiques and Chapters, children can hit Toys 'R' Us, and teenagers can catch a movie at Metropolis or the funky clothes stores. Metrotown Centre is located at 4800 Kingsway in Burnaby.

RICHMOND CENTRE: Presentation is everything. The multi-coloured marble floor—think warm creams, dusty pinks, jade greens and shiny blacks—gives this mall a palatial feel. Richmond Centre boasts the usual boutiques and chain stores, but as you slide your feet over the gleaming floors, you can imagine yourself transported to a world where White Spot is fine dining. Richmond Centre is located at 6551 No. 3 Road in Richmond.

KIDS ONLY MARKET: Set in a ketchup-and-mustard building, Kids Mall is a primary-coloured dream come true for the whole family. Children love exploring a building filled with toys, games and specialities such as an eyeglasses store for miniature bookworms. If you and your little ones get hungry while shopping, check out Woofles dog deli next door. Kids Only Market is located on Granville Island, underneath the Granville Street Bridge.

PACIFIC CENTRE: This is the mother of all Vancouver malls. This gigantic shopping centre has stores that sell everything at all price ranges, from dollar stores to exclusive department stores. Multi-levelled with towering fountains, glass skylights and potted plants, this is the place for the serious shopper. It's air-conditioned, sub-street level location make it a treat to visit on hot summer days. Pacific Centre is located at 700 West Georgia in Vancouver.

SURREY PLACE: This giant mall is an oasis in the middle of farm territory. Inside, it's an entire city with two solid floors of stores and enough skylights to make you feel like you're out shopping in the fields. Surrey Place is located at 102nd Avenue and King George Highway in Surrey.

YAOHAN CENTRE: This is Vancouver's most exotic mall. Skip your gourmet blend for a day and order some coconut milk to wash down a plate of Szechuan beef at this Asian mecca of a shopping centre. A reasonably priced food court will satisfy any Asian food fanatic, and once you're here, you can take a look at the Chinese art and Asian grocery store. Yaohan Centre is located at 3700 No. 3 Road in Richmond.

GRANVILLE STREET MALL: An outdoor mall in the truest sense of the word, this pedestrian-traffic only section of Granville Street has undergone many attempts at reformation in recent years. Newly refurbished theatres, such as the Commodore Ballroom, herald the beginnings of upscale development. Check out the funky stores along the street, such as Golden Age Collectibles, which has a great supply of old movie posters and comics.

SINCLAIR CENTRE: Housed in what once was the Post Office, this mall is an architectural anomaly and it transports the shopper straight into the 19th century with its chiselled awnings and art-gallery feel. The upscale boutiques in this mall are out of the price range of the usual bargain hunter. If you're looking for a quiet place to shop, though, Sunday afternoon crowds usually bypass this quiet little treasure. Sinclair Centre is located at 757 West Hastings in downtown Vancouver.

CAPILANO MALL: Hibernate for a few hours in this softly lit mall on the North Shore. Strolling couples give it a laid-back atmosphere and a pair of three-storey tall totem poles make for interesting interior design. This mall boasts a great food court with more healthy alternatives than the usual fast-food fare. Capilano Mall is located at 935 Marine Drive in North Vancouver.

GREAT MOVIE THEATRES

By David Spaner

There was a time when every Vancouver neighbourhood had a movie theatre and downtown had "motion picture palaces" as glitzy as opera houses. Nowadays, movies are usually watched in barren rooms in malls or super-multiplexes. But some of the Lower Mainland's great old theatres survive, and a few of the newer ones are pleasant surprises. Here are ten of the best.

HOLLYWOOD: From its balcony to its ticket booth to even its tinselly name, this theatre has meant the movies to generations of Vancouver residents. What makes the Hollywood so great is that it survives as a simple, ordinary 1930s theatre, the only one in the area to enter the 21st century pretty much as it was on opening night. This is a theatre with thick red velvet curtains on washroom doors, and ashtrays, chandeliers and other furnishings that haven't changed since the place opened in 1935. The Hollywood is located at 2123 West Broadway in Vancouver.

RIDGE: This theatre looks like something built in Los Angeles during its post-war boom years when people across North America were California dreaming. The Ridge has lived several lives, opening as a first-run neighbourhood theatre (where *The Sound of Music* played the longest run in the city's history), complete with a crying room. Then it was a revival house with great double bills. Now it features foreign and independent releases. The Ridge is located at 3131 Arbutus Street in Vancouver.

PACIFIC CINEMATHEQUE: Nothing fancy here, but enter this sparse room and you're transported to a New York art house cinema. Pacific Cinematheque offers an eclectic mix of ethnic festivals and tributes to filmmakers such as Alfred Hitchcock and Preston Sturges. Pacific Cinematheque is located at 1131 Howe Street in Vancouver.

HILLCREST DRIVE-IN: The last of the drive-in theatres in the Lower Mainland, this is the place for those who want to experience a night out at the movies. Pack your pillows and blankets and relive the charm of fussing around with a sound system, loading up at a cholesterol-infested concession building and doing whatever else it is people have always done at drive-ins. The Hillcrest Drive-in is located at 18694 Fraser Highway in Surrey.

FIFTH AVENUE: The Fifth Avenue is one of those buildings like the Ford Centre that looks nicer on the outside than it does on the claustrophobic inside. But this almost-new five-screen venue isn't on this list for its aesthetics. It's here because of a wonderful mixture of first-run movies—foreign, offbeat Hollywood releases, art films, independents…oh, and the free parking. The Fifth Avenue is located at 2110 Burrard Street, Vancouver.

PARK & TILFORD: Located next to Lion's Gate Movie Studio, Park & Tilford boasts a spacious lobby lined with mini-movie houses. It's one of the best examples of a Cineplex in town, and after the movie you can stroll through the Park and Tilford Gardens for a bracing dose of reality. The Park & Tilford is located at 200-333 Brooksbank Street, North Vancouver.

VANCOUVER EAST CINEMA: Although this nondescript building is still labelled Far East, it shows second-run features and foreign films. It has cheap prices and is a favourite with many people in East Vancouver. The Vancouver East Cinema is located at 2290 Commercial Drive in Vancouver.

SILVERCITY RIVERPORT: This was the first of the recently constructed theatres in the Lower Mainland with a spectacular new perspective—seating so high and steep that viewers actually look down at the screen. Comfortable chairs and extra leg room spoil movie-goers for ordinary theatres. If you're heading out to see a long movie, this is your best bet for comfort. SilverCity Riverport is located at 14211 Entertainment Way, Richmond.

CAPRICE: Kind of tattered now, this Tsawwassen theatre is here as the representative of first-generation mall theatres, built long before they were mega and multi and all -plexed out. A box-like building separate from its mall with only one screen and few adornments, it shows first-run movies. The Caprice is located at 1259-56th Street, Tsawwassen.

VARSITY: Located in the closest thing to a university district in the Lower Mainland, the Varsity is a large, comfortable, single-screen theatre that has shown cerebral film fare for decades. The Varsity was home to an early film festival that helped inspire the current annual Vancouver International Film Festival. Margot Kidder was an usher here. The Varsity is located at 4375 West 10th Avenue in Vancouver.

GREAT PLACES TO SKI AND SNOWBOARD

By Staff Reporters

British Columbia certainly has no shortage of great skiing mountains. Hey, we're not bragging, but the truth is, if you're looking for fantastic snowboarding or skiing, making the decision where to go is going to be your toughest challenge. Just to help you out (and take the opportunity to boast about our local natural wonders), we've assembled a list of ten great places to ski or snowboard, all within a day's drive from Vancouver. We could have added more, but that would have been overkill.

LOCAL MOUNTAINS: We are certainly blessed with them. But which one should you bless with your business? Everyone loves the gondola going up to—and coming down from—Grouse Mountain in North Vancouver. There's nothing like the snowshoeing in the backwoods of Mount Seymour in North Vancouver. But, for the complete big-mountain experience in our backyard, it's hard not to be partial to Cypress. It has the greatest variety of runs of the local mountains, the view from the top on a clear day is priceless, and the snowboard park is cool. The prices at all three mountains are a sweet deal compared to anywhere else. Cypress Mountain is located off Exit 8 on Highway 99 in West Vancouver.

WHISTLER/BLACKCOMB: For the sake of originality, we decided listing Whistler/Blackcomb as number 2 would make a nice change. The truth is, there are few mountains in the world as remarkable as these. Whistler's got it all—phenomenal terrain, phenomenal village, phenomenal growth (check out the newer lifts), and you can get two mountains for the price of one. Check out the lift ticket deals that are offered through 7-11 stores throughout the ski season for a great price. To get to Whistler/Blackcomb, head north on the Sea-to-Sky Highway (Highway 99).

SUN PEAKS: When you're looking for Olympic skiers schussing down the slopes, Sun Peaks is the place to be. Located north of Kamloops, Sun Peaks is home to Nancy Greene, former Canadian Olympic champion and legend. Nancy can be found on the slopes during the time she steals away from her busy schedule as a resort owner/operator. When you get off the mountain, head to the village's skating rink. It's like being a small-town pond all over again. To get to Kamloops, take Highway 99 to Hope, then the Coquahalla Highway to Kamloops.

MOUNT BAKER: We're not sure if the Guinness Book of World Records confirmed it or not, but Washington State's Mount Baker enjoyed a record snowfall in 1998. Baker's that mountain that seems to loom over the Fraser Valley, and it's really that impressive up close. There's tons of snow—so much, in fact, that they have to dig out the chairlifts sometimes. You can't beat the ride up to Baker. It's much like the Matterhorn ride at Disneyland, only you've got to put on the chains. Mount Baker is located 90 kilometres (56 miles) east of Bellingham on State Highway 542, two hours from Vancouver.

RED MOUNTAIN: It's getting harder and harder in British Columbia to find a mountain that hasn't been the beneficiary of a bundle of media attention and mass commercialism. Then there's Red Mountain in Rossland. It's steep, it's funky, and it's the spawning ground of Olympians. Canadian Olympic and World Cup champions Nancy Greene and Kerrin Lee Gartner learned to ski here. Rossland is located in the Kootenay region of British Columbia. To get to Rossland and Red Mountain, take Highway 99 to Hope, and Highway 1 to Rossland.

BLUE RIVER HELI-SKIING: Heli-skiing is something most of us will never do. It's expensive and it's…expensive. Then again, you only live once and if you're only in British Columbia this one time, you should try Mike Wiegele's heli-skiing at Blue River. Try an elevation unmatched anywhere else in British Columbia, a correspondingly huge vertical, and you can ride high on virgin powder. Follower up with a relaxing stay in the five-star lodge, featured in a recent Warren Miller movie, and you've got one of the greatest experiences on earth. Phone 250-673-8381 for more information.

BIG WHITE: It's the snow. That's one of the more recent marketing slogans for Big White, near Kelowna, and it's no lie. This mountain, just over four hours from Vancouver, spends most of the winter buried under the white stuff. Not only is Big White known for its powder, but it's got those funky snow ghosts—trees so encased in snow that they no longer look like trees.

SILVER STAR: If you're visiting Kelowna or Vernon, you could spend one day at Big White and another at Silver Star. Everyone raves about the village, which is tiny but quaint in an 1890s-themed, no-Whistler crowds kind of way. Try the Putnam Creek side of the mountain. It's virtually all black diamond. Kelowna and Vernon are located in the Okanagan region of British Columbia. To reach Big White or Silver Star, take Highway 99 to Hope. Continue on the Coquahalla Highway and follow the signs to Kelowna.

MOUNT WASHINGTON: Vancouver Island seems so flat and dry, which makes Mount Washington, near Courtenay, hard to explain. But with near-record snowfalls in recent years, they have actually had to close a few times because of too much snow. Mount Washington has some superb runs, and it's ski club is home to Alison Forsyth, a slalom specialist who is doing very well on the World Cup circuit. Ferries leave from Tsawwassan daily to Vancouver Island. Follow the Island Highway up to Courtenay.

PANORAMA: Located outside of Cranbrook, in the Kootenay region of British Columbia, Panorama has some of the best fall lines around, which make for better turns. The mountain is steep enough for experts—it used to host World Cup runs. It's also got some great cruising runs. The funky, small village features the classic T-Bar Lounge at the base. To get to Cranbrook, follow Highway 99 to Hope. Take the Trans Canada Highway to Golden and follow the signs to Cranbook.

GREAT STREETS IN VANCOUVER

BY DANA GEE

Need a break from the usual tourist routine? Looking for a taste of the real Vancouver and a clue to what constitutes "West Coast Chic?" Take a break from your routine and make a mini-vacation out of a visit to another neighbourhood. When you've chosen a locale to visit, live a little and venture out of your usual comfort zone. Give yourself a quest, such as finding the perfect antique fireplace or the cheapest paper blinds. Here are ten Lower Mainland streets we love to linger on. Enjoy!

COMMERCIAL DRIVE: From the coffee shops to the cantinas, the Drive (as it is affectionately nicknamed by locals) offers up a healthy serving of cultural cool. Traditionalists aim for Joe's Café for coffee and Nick's Spaghetti House for pasta. Nouveau street strollers lap up the counter-culture feel of the Latin Quarter, Havana or Bukowski's. Shopping is as eclectic as the neighbourhood people. For the right knitted hat or beaded necklace, check out Rastawares. Explore the artistic offerings at Doctor Vigari's for an interesting item to adorn your mantle or a unique wedding gift.

ROBSON STREET: It's a shopaholic's dream come true. This savvy stretch offers consumers everything from finger-licking good fudge to fashionable Fila footwear. If you've come into some money and fancy a day of pure decadence, take a stroll down Robson Street. Get a makeover at the hip, oh-so-London Tony and Guy Salon. Get some new clothes at trendy FCUT, BeBe or Club Monaco. Pick up the perfect wedding shower present at Chachkas. A word of warning: Sunshine and holidays bring out every shopper in the known universe. Be prepared to merely plod along during peak times.

MONCTON STREET IN STEVESTON: Quaint crafts and interesting antiques are peppered in among yummy fish'n'chips restaurants, markets and a marine and hardware store. For seafood shopping, try Steveston Fish Shoppe or wander south a block to the docks, a great place to stroll or troll for fresh fish right off the boats.

GRANVILLE ISLAND: It's hard to avoid this weekend mecca as a popular place to putter about. Fruits and vegetable stands are top drawer. After loading up on fibre-packed lettuce and calcium-rich kale, toss a few gobstoppers from Candy Kitchen and something gooey from A la Mode Bakery into your bags for good measure. Try on the latest in headgear at Edie's Hats or pick out something shiny from one of the many Northwest Coastal artists who sell through the Wickanninnish Gallery. However, like Robson Street, busy holiday times are a recipe for frustration, so proceed with patience.

MARINE DRIVE IN WHITE ROCK: If you like crowds and a kind of carnival atmosphere, this is the place to go on a sunny Saturday or Sunday. The place is a zoo with lots of cruising action, as well as families with children buying fish and chips from Cottage Lunch and other little eateries along East Beach. The mile-plus long promenade joins west and east beaches. There are dozens of good restaurants with outdoor seating along Marine Drive, ranging from high-end French to the no-pretensions family eateries.

MAIN STREET: From folk art to fine art to retro 1950s appliances, Main Street has it all when it comes to decorating with style. The undisputed antique capital of the city, Main from Broadway up offers a whole day's worth of browsing. If you want a little more information before you start to shop, peruse the selection of books on antiques at the Blue Heron at 19th and Main. When you spot an antique you like, don't be afraid to haggle.

CHINATOWN: Keefer and East Pender Streets offer an abundance of Asian treats and delicacies. Prices are good and the variety is spectacular. If you don't get going until lunchtime, start your day off with dim sum. Anything from exotic teas to sea cucumbers to dried seahorses to whole barbecued piglets can be found on these two bustling boulevards. Chinatown is a great place to find cheap kitchen stuff and nifty gifts.

GLOVER ROAD IN FORT LANGLEY: If cute is your calling, then this strip of country life is perfect. Exit north off Highway 1 at 232nd Street and follow the signs to Fort Langley. Park and walk. Start with a trip through the old cemetery, then browse away the day. Budget time for Gasoline Alley Antiques Mall and Village Antiques Mall. If you're really lucky, you may catch one of the many auctions held at the old city hall. A good way to end the day is a pub snack and a cool one at the Fort Langley Pub on the banks of the Fraser River. Again, if you're lucky, you may be in time to get in on one of the meat draws.

SOUTHLANDS: Now, except for nearby golf club snack bars and pro-shops, the food, refreshment and shopping factors are non-existent. But what it lacks in amenities it makes up for in vistas. Drive straight down Blenheim and park by the tennis courts next to the river. Follow the path that heads west separating the river from Point Grey Golf Course. The path, which leads along the river down to the edge of the Musqueam Indian Reservation, offers walkers an up-close look at a busy part of the mighty Fraser. A word of warning:

This is horse country, so watch out for people riding along the sides of roads and the bridle trail that runs along the river.

BROADWAY FROM BALSAM TO ALMA: As far as neighbourhoods go, the only thing missing from this stretch are a butcher and a seafood shop. With these, residents of this area would never have to venture out into another scary, big-box store ever again. Minerva's is a well-stocked Greek market and the handful of green grocers offer a wide range of fruits and vegetables at well below supermarket prices. At the heart of this strip is the magnificent Hollywood Theatre. The pre-war picture house offers second-run movies at cut-rate prices in a grand setting.

INDEX

INDEX

INDEX